THE PROFESSOR
AND THE PARSON

ALSO BY ADAM SISMAN

A. J. P. Taylor: A Biography

Boswell's Presumptuous Task

Wordsworth and Coleridge: The Friendship

Hugh Trevor-Roper

John le Carré

THE PROFESSOR

and

THE PARSON

A Story of Desire,
Deceit, and Defrocking

ADAM SISMAN

COUNTERPOINT
Berkeley, California

The Professor and the Parson

Copyright © 2019 by Adam Sisman
First published in Great Britain in 2019 by PROFILE BOOKS LTD, 3
Holford Yard, Bevin Way, London, wc1x 9hd, www.profilebooks.com

First Counterpoint hardcover edition: 2020

ISBN: 978-1-64009-328-7

The Library of Congress Cataloging-in-Publication Data is available.

Jacket design by Richard Ljoenes
Book design by MacGuru Ltd

COUNTERPOINT
2560 Ninth Street, Suite 318
Berkeley, CA 94710
www.counterpointpress.com

Printed in the United States of America
Distributed by Publishers Group West

1 3 5 7 9 10 8 6 4 2

For Felicity

'It shows, my dear Watson, that we are dealing with an exceptionally astute and dangerous man. The Rev. Dr Shlessinger, missionary from South America, is none other than Holy Peters, one of the most unscrupulous rascals that Australia has ever evolved – and for a young country it has turned out some very finished types. His particular speciality is the beguiling of lonely ladies by playing upon their religious feelings, and his so-called wife, an English woman named Fraser, is a worthy helpmate.'

from 'The Disappearance of Lady Frances Carfax' by Arthur Conan Doyle

Contents

THE PROFESSOR
AND THE PARSON

Prologue

On 25 November 2005 a man died at Kettering General Hospital, Northamptonshire. The death certificate was registered four days later. The person registering the death was Ann Barbara Peters, widow of the deceased. The dead man's name was given as Robert Peters. He was described as a retired university lecturer. The certificate gave his date of birth as 11 August 1928, which made him seventy-seven at the time of his death.

None of these details was true.

Introduction

I happened upon the story of Robert Peters while writing a biography of the historian Hugh Trevor-Roper. Like most people, I had not heard of Peters before. I first noticed his name on the cover of a thick folder, inscribed by fountain pen in Trevor-Roper's lucid, distinctive hand. The folder was among the papers in his study at the Old Rectory, sometimes unkindly described as the only nice house in Didcot. After Trevor-Roper's death in 2003, the Old Rectory remained silent and uninhabited for several years, its contents largely undisturbed. In winter it was bitterly cold. I would go there occasionally to work on these papers, trying to keep warm in coat and gloves until the heating took the edge off the chill. On at least one occasion I slept in Trevor-Roper's bed; his clothes still hung in the wardrobe, and there were still books on the bedside table, including of course a volume of Horace. His was no ordinary archive; among the more conventional records of an academic historian was correspondence with some of the most senior officers in British intelligence, and other documents relating to Trevor-Roper's wartime service with MI6 – including an adjutant's ledger of Hitler's appointments, no doubt pocketed during Trevor-Roper's exploration of the ruined and partially flooded bunker in the autumn of 1945.

Eventually the contents of his study were removed to Christ Church. As the movers lifted one of the archive boxes into the waiting van, a Luger dropped out.

My biography of Trevor-Roper was published in 2010. As the book relates, Trevor-Roper met Peters in Oxford in the late 1950s. Trevor-Roper was then a professor, and Peters a student reading for a postgraduate degree. The professor agreed to see him, to hear Peters complain that he was being persecuted. Like so many others before and since, Trevor-Roper believed the elaborate tale that Peters told him, until it began to collapse under the weight of contrary evidence. Once he realised that Peters had been lying, Trevor-Roper was sufficiently intrigued to want to know more. He investigated further, and was startled by what he discovered. As a responsible academic, he was appalled by Peters's success in outwitting the authorities; but as an individual who delighted in the *comédie humaine*, he could not help being amused by it. He took a malicious glee in the discomfiture of those whom Peters had fooled. Peters's ploys exposed the innocence of some, and the pomposity of others.

Trevor-Roper began to keep a dossier on Peters, which he would maintain for the next quarter of a century. A network of informants, in different countries and in different spheres of life, kept the professor abreast of the latest antics of 'our old friend'. It was this bulky dossier that I found in Trevor-Roper's archive while conducting research into his life. In my biography I drew on the dossier to write a brief account of Trevor-Roper's initial brush with Peters. But this was only the beginning; most of what he learned about Peters remained untold. The professor was urged to write a book about the bogus parson, and was tempted to do so; but he hesitated, deterred by the threat of a defamation suit while Peters yet lived. He continued to collect information about Peters, but for now he preferred to write about another extraordinary fraudster, this one safely dead: the eccentric Sinologist Sir Edmund Backhouse. Though their backgrounds were utterly different, Trevor-Roper recognised similarities between the characters of Peters and Backhouse. The deceitfulness of such men was matched by their gall.

In 2017, while I was revisiting Trevor-Roper's archive, now safely stowed in Oxford, it occurred to me to consider writing about Peters myself. Trevor-Roper's dossier was my starting point, but I soon found another substantial file on Peters, kept by successive Presidents of Magdalen, the Oxford college to which Peters had belonged at the time when he met Trevor-Roper; and then another bulky folder, in the Cambridge University Library, of material on Peters assembled by a former Regius Professor of Divinity. I contacted a retired clergyman, then in hospital in the last stages of his final illness, who ensured that I received his own dossier, which he jokingly referred to as 'The Life and Crimes of Robert Parkin Peters'. Other documents came my way through a variety of sources; one of those with whom I made contact had contemplated writing a book about Peters himself. I am sure that there is more material to be found: not least at Lambeth Palace, where there is said to be a filing cabinet stuffed with papers on Peters. My attempts to storm the palace have been repulsed. The official line is that 'clergy disciplinary files' cannot be made available to scholars until thirty years after the subject's death – in this case until 2035, and I cannot wait that long. My argument that Robert Peters had not been an Anglican clergyman since 1955 was met with a stony silence: the door has remained firmly shut. Of course I understand why such files are sensitive; but if the story of Robert Peters shows anything, it is that swindlers benefit from the reluctance of individuals and institutions to reveal that they have been swindled. Secrecy benefits the criminal. In this instance, so far as I am aware, the Church of England has little, if anything, of which to be ashamed, though perhaps something of which to be embarrassed. Earlier custodians of Lambeth Palace had been keen to spread the word about Peters's misdemeanours, but the incumbents prefer to keep mum. It cannot possibly do any harm, and it might well do good, for Lambeth Palace to make an exception to its own arbitrary rule. But there is no reasoning with the bureaucratic mind.

Other avenues of enquiry also led nowhere. Perhaps understandably, some of the women who had been deceived by Peters were reluctant to talk to me; and I felt reluctant to press them. While aware that there must be more to be discovered about Peters, I felt that I had to stop somewhere, or I would never finish. As Trevor-Roper himself remarked, at a similar point in his study of a different subject, there is a law of diminishing returns; and 'if a problem will not yield to a direct assault, it may be wisdom to pass it by and tackle another, which may indirectly serve our purpose, rather than lay a long and futile siege to an impregnable fortress.'

It was clear to me from the start that a conventional biography was not the best form for such a subject. For one thing, Peters was such an inveterate liar that it was impossible to believe a single word that he wrote or said: even the most mundane facts would need to be verified independently. Thus, for example, he consistently lied about the year of his birth, providing different dates at different times. Trevor-Roper compiled what he called a 'curriculum vitae', a true chronology of Peters's life, in contrast to the many fallacious curricula vitae that Peters composed in the course of his career. (He would sometimes refer to this as the 'Revised Version', an allusion to the revised version of the King James Bible issued in the nineteenth century.) I have appended at the end of this book an updated chronology, as a guide to readers who may find Peters's often tortuous progression confusing.

Studying Peters is like tracking a particle in a cloud chamber: usually one cannot see the man himself, but only the path he left behind. I realised early on in the process that Peters could only be known from the outside: his inner thoughts and feelings were hidden, and would almost certainly remain so, however much I might discover about him otherwise. Indeed, it seemed to me likely that he barely knew himself, because had he done, he surely could not have acted as he did. His motives could only be deduced from his behaviour. Nevertheless I have attempted a brief character sketch as a form of conclusion.

This book is divided into three parts. The first part describes the initial encounter between the professor and the parson, and Trevor-Roper's dawning appreciation that Peters was not what he pretended to be. It is drawn largely from a document written by Trevor-Roper soon afterwards, while his memory was still fresh. The dossier itself is the basis of the second part, the core of the story, as Trevor-Roper pursued Peters over a twenty-five-year period. The third part of the book describes what happened to Peters after Trevor-Roper gave up the pursuit, and what I discovered when I took it up again, half a lifetime later. Like a detective re-examining an old case, I have been frustrated to find that parts of the story are now irretrievable. But to compensate for that which has been lost, I have been able to discover much that is new.

Some readers, alarmed by Peters's success as a con man, may feel that this story is a cautionary tale. But my purpose has been to entertain, not to instruct. I hope that many readers will find the book as enjoyable to read as it has been to write.

PART I

1958–9

ONE

In which the professor meets the parson and hears his history

The letter itself has not survived in the file; nor has the envelope. All we can be sure of is that on a November day in 1958 a letter arrived, addressed to the Regius Professor of Modern History.

The Regius Professor was Hugh Trevor-Roper, who had been appointed to this post, the most senior within the faculty, the previous year. As such he was correctly addressed not as 'Professor', but as 'Regius'.

Still only forty-four years old, Trevor-Roper was then at the height of his powers. Though very short-sighted, with thick pebble spectacles, he was celebrated for his forensic powers of enquiry, which he had exhibited as an MI6 officer, in his official investigation into the fate of the Führer. He pursued evidence with the same avidity as he had pursued foxes – until he fell from a horse and broke his back. Witty, clever and confident, even arrogant, he was equally at ease in common rooms or drawing rooms: he mixed easily in high society, and in 1954 had married Lady Alexandra, eldest daughter of Field Marshal Earl Haig. In

'Wielding a cruel pen': Hugh Trevor-Roper in
his Christ Church rooms in the 1950s.

1947 he had made his name with his bestselling book *The Last
Days of Hitler*, which drew on his wartime intelligence work.
From the proceeds he was able to buy a grey Bentley, which he
parked ostentatiously in Christ Church's Tom Quad. Now he
was writing a big book on the English Civil War, which, it was
confidently predicted, would cement his reputation as one of the
leading scholars of his generation. He was also enjoying a long-
running feud with the most formidable of foes, Evelyn Waugh.
'There is nothing so exhilarating as a good battle, I find,' he
wrote to his brother-in-law, after successfully defending himself
against a prosecution for dangerous driving: 'especially if one
wins it!' Wielding a cruel pen, he was a daunting opponent,
feared for his merciless demolition of historians who failed to
meet his scholarly standards. Unsurprisingly he made enemies,

within and without the university; his success bred jealousy and resentment. But such feelings were not uncommon in Oxford, where enforced proximity over long years could sharpen dislike into loathing.

The letter came from a Miss Gibson, who lived in North Oxford. As daughter of the late Nuffield Reader in Pathology, she was connected with the university, albeit indirectly, and therefore had some claim on the attention of its senior officers. She referred to her lodgers, a married couple. This pair, she said, were suffering, both in their health and in their studies, as a result of 'vindictive persecution from outside the university'; and she appealed to the Regius Professor, as one of the most senior members of the faculty in which both worked, to help them.

Trevor-Roper vaguely recalled the couple, a Mr and Mrs Peters, who had appeared at his seminar in early modern history back in the summer. Both were graduate students, working for B.Litt. degrees:* he on the archdeaconry of St Albans in the sixteenth century, she on the eighteenth-century press. Like all members of the university, each was attached to a college: he to Magdalen, she to Lady Margaret Hall. They had attended his seminar for a fortnight, and then appeared no more. There was nothing particularly mysterious in this absence; graduate students came and went, following their own interests and specialities wherever these led.

Trevor-Roper telephoned Miss Gibson and cautiously enquired whether her lodgers might not be suffering from a

---

* The B.Litt. (Bachelor of Letters) is a higher degree, no longer awarded at Oxford and most other universities.

persecution complex. She was adamant that they were not. In a voice trembling with emotion, she begged him to help 'these dear people'. Trevor-Roper agreed to see Peters at his office in the history faculty at noon the next day.

They met for an hour. Peters was a small, chubby-cheeked, bespectacled man with thinning hair and an earnest manner, who spoke with a slight lisp. He told Trevor-Roper that he was thirty-four, though he looked older. He had spent some years in America; and there, he said, had been ordained priest by Bishop Bayne of the diocese of Olympia, in Washington State. Throughout the interview he made a favourable impression, answering questions sensibly and readily providing details of names, places and approximate dates. Using a fountain pen, Trevor-Roper took notes on a sheet of lined foolscap. It did not occur to him to question his visitor's veracity.

When Peters told the professor that he was being persecuted 'in the most unaccountable manner' by the Bishop of Oxford, the Right Reverend Harry Carpenter, Trevor-Roper's interest was immediately awakened; here, perhaps, was an opportunity for him to make mischief. He relished sparring with authority, with the Church authorities perhaps most of all. In part this was personal, to do with his own violent reaction against religion as a young man. In part it was circumstantial, for he had been surrounded by clergymen for most of his Oxford career. Trevor-Roper had been an undergraduate and then a young don at Christ Church, which was (and remains) a unique combination of college and cathedral, known as 'the House' after its Latin name, *Aedes Christi*, the House of Christ. The head of the college is the Dean of the Cathedral, supported by six canon professors. As a result there has always been within Christ Church a tension between the sacred and the secular. Trevor-Roper's relations with his clerical colleagues were generally cordial, but teasing: he took pleasure in anything that caused them discomfort, while they generally tolerated him with Christian forbearance. His first book, a biographical study of Archbishop Laud, had made him notorious for his anticlerical quips. 'Laud's clerical biographers,' he had written, 'since they approach him on their knees, are naturally unable to see very far.' He had mocked the established Church as 'an unmolested cipher, neither loved nor hated, and approached with the decent, if meaningless, reverence allowed to the dead'. But Trevor-Roper's jibes were not limited to Anglicans; he dealt it out to both High and Low, scoffing at Catholics as credulous fanatics and dissenters as joyless Puritans.

Peters explained that his friend the Reverend Leon Janes, vicar of St Barnabas (an imposing Italianate church in Jericho),* had invited him to officiate there, and that he had been eager to oblige; but being a punctilious person, he had thought that he should obtain permission from the Bishop of Oxford before doing so. Luckily he had happened to meet Bishop Carpenter over a college dinner one night at Keble,† had broached the subject then and had renewed his request by calling on him at home. The bishop had seemed willing to grant his wish, though he had alluded to certain differences of doctrine between the Church of England and the Episcopal Church in America,

---

* St Barnabas was founded in the nineteenth century by supporters of the Oxford Movement and has maintained the Anglo-Catholic traditions of its founders to this day.
† Carpenter was an honorary Fellow of Keble, having been Warden of the college before being made bishop; undergraduates there knew him as 'the Carp'.

which made it necessary for him to discuss the matter with the American bishop who had ordained Peters. Fortunately that very bishop, the Bishop of Olympia, would be in England imminently, to attend the Lambeth Conference.

At first, so Peters recounted, everything had gone swimmingly. Bishop Carpenter had gone up to London during the Lambeth Conference, had discussed the matter with his Episcopalian brother, Bishop Bayne, and all was now settled. Shortly after his return to Oxford, in a chance meeting in the street, he had spoken to Peters and had confirmed that he was now free to officiate within the diocese. And so the hitherto hesitant Peters had mounted the pulpit of St Barnabas and boldly preached the word of God to an attentive congregation. And then he had done so again, and again – until one Sunday evening, when, in an apparently inexplicable volte-face, the bishop had telephoned the Reverend Mr Janes and instructed him that on no account should Peters be allowed to officiate any longer at St Barnabas, or anywhere else in the diocese. The vicar had protested, but the bishop was firm. He denied ever having met Peters and disclaimed any knowledge of him.

Humiliated and insulted, Peters protested to Trevor-Roper that he had done everything he ought to have done in obtaining permission from the bishop before preaching, though he admitted that he had received nothing in writing to that effect. Now he feared that the bishop had some prejudice against him. Evidence had come his way of the arbitrary proceedings of Bishop Carpenter, of his instability of purpose and capricious memory, of his unjust practices, of his bias against virtuous parsons from America.

'What has all this to do with me?' asked Trevor-Roper. Peters replied that it had a bearing on his work for his B.Litt. degree. He had been labouring hard. His supervisor, Miss Kathleen

Major, a medieval historian who also happened to be Principal of St Hilda's College, was pleased with his progress. He planned soon to submit his dissertation to the faculty board. The B.Litt. was of great importance to him. And now, at the last moment, the shadow of the prelate had fallen between him and his objective. He feared that the bishop might intervene to prevent the board from granting him a degree.

Trevor-Roper sought to reassure him. The bishop had nothing to do with the board. The only way in which it could be persuaded not to admit him to a degree would be if his college, Magdalen, refused to sponsor his application. 'But that,' exclaimed Peters, 'is precisely what the bishop may now achieve!' There was evidence that the bishop had slandered him to the college authorities. The President of Magdalen* had sent for Peters, and had asked a series of disquieting questions. 'Do you think,' the President had asked at one point, 'that anyone has been impersonating you?' Peters had been unsettled by the interview, though no accusations had been laid against him. He asked himself what lay behind it. Why had the President, a busy man, busier still since the beginning of that academic year, when he had taken on the extra responsibilities of Vice-Chancellor, summoned him? Plainly he had been measuring up Peters against some information from outside. Where had this information come from? Once Peters asked himself this question, the unspoken purpose of the interview had become obvious: he had

---

* Heads of Oxford colleges are known by a variety of titles. The head of Magdalen is President; the head of St Hilda's is Principal; and the head of Christ Church is Dean. Other heads of college are known as Master, Rector, Warden and Provost.

been denounced by the bishop, and the President was fishing for the truth. If that were so, where would it end? The bishop had shown by his actions that he did not think Peters a proper person to preach at St Barnabas. Might not the bishop succeed in persuading the President that Peters was not a proper person to be a member of the college, and therefore not qualified to hold a degree?

Trevor-Roper offered to mediate. It was an odd story, but the man was visibly anxious and deserved reassurance. The professor saw no reason to doubt his account. Asked how he had come to be accepted at Magdalen the previous year, Peters told Trevor-Roper that he had a first-class degree from the University of London, and had been recommended for postgraduate work by two of the senior historians there, Sir John Neale and Joel Hurstfield, both eminent specialists in the history of Elizabethan England and men whom Trevor-Roper knew and respected. Altogether his references seemed excellent. Trevor-Roper told Peters that he knew the President of Magdalen well and would have an informal word with him about the matter – which, he was confident, would be speedily resolved. Though his interviewee did not seem enthusiastic about this proposal, Trevor-Roper swept his diffidence aside. He dismissed Peters and went home for lunch.

In so far as he thought about it at all, Trevor-Roper assumed that Peters's fears were groundless. Presumably the matter arose from a misunderstanding, which could be easily resolved. It did not seem to him particularly urgent. Three weeks passed before he found the time to call on the President, the Scots art historian T. S. R. Boase, known to his friends as 'Tom'.

A bachelor, Boase was a large, energetic, fastidious man who worked rapidly and with precision; in his beliefs he was a firm Christian. He received Trevor-Roper in his spartan lodgings, opposite the main entrance to the college on 'the High'. The President listened intently, kneading the back of one hand with the long fingers of the other as Trevor-Roper related what Peters had said. Afterwards Boase told Trevor-Roper that all this was quite new to him. He had never spoken to the Bishop of Oxford. He had never made the remark about impersonation. He sent for a worn manila folder, from which he extracted evidence that told quite a different story.

Peters had been a last-minute applicant to Magdalen in the previous year, 1957, so late that some of the formalities had been overlooked. On being asked by the college authorities to provide a certificate of his undergraduate degree, Peters had apologised for not doing so, explaining that it was among his belongings at his parents' house in Cumberland; he had promised to produce it by the date of the matriculation ceremony on 5 December, but never did, and the request had been forgotten. He had arrived in Oxford midway through the Michaelmas term.

He seemed to fit in well enough, though not much was seen of him in college. A member of Magdalen who knew him slightly would later describe him as 'a meek and mild sort of chap, and very pleasant to talk to'. He never wore a dog collar, so that nobody in college had any reason to suppose that he was, or had ever been, anything but a layman. In fact he had initiated a conversation with the college Dean about the possibility of seeking ordination 'at some stage in the future'.

As postgraduates often do, Peters had chosen to supplement his income by offering to coach undergraduates. One of these,

Robert Peters and Marie Baillie on their wedding-day, 22 March 1958.

a student of Trinity, may have smelt a rat: in any case, he had
the presence of mind to enquire of the Registrar whether his
prospective tutor had, as he claimed, a degree with first-class
honours from the University of London. The answer stated that
he had not. Had this information been more widely distributed
at the time, much trouble would have been saved.

In his second term at Oxford, Peters had courted and won
the hand of Miss Marie Baillie, an attractive young woman from
New Zealand, a postgraduate at Lady Margaret Hall and herself
studying for a B.Litt. By special permission of the President, a
service of blessing was held in the chapel of Magdalen College,
following the wedding itself at the local register office. Boase had
regretfully refused the bride's request that the bells in Magdalen
Tower should be rung, explaining that they were 'very over-
powering' in hall, where 'collections' – oral assessments of the

undergraduates' work by the President and the tutors – were due to be held at the same time. A champagne reception followed the ceremony, attended by (so it was later reported) heads of colleges and other distinguished guests.

Peters was sensible of his status as a member of Magdalen, one of the oldest and grandest of the Oxford colleges (though perhaps not quite as grand as Christ Church). Three weeks after the wedding, he wrote a Pooterish letter to an Oxford estate agent who had apparently failed to let the newlyweds a flat. 'You evidently do not realise that members of this university are not accustomed to being treated in this manner by business people,' he complained, 'or for that matter being addressed in tones of familiarity by office staff, as happened yesterday when one of your staff addressed me as "old boy".' He warned that he intended to report the incident to the Oxford Chamber of Commerce, 'and, if need be, to the Board of Trade'.

Not long after this, the Registrar of the college had received a letter from the Law Notes Lending Library in London. The library had been unable to contact Peters concerning a book he had borrowed three months earlier. The Registrar forwarded the letter to Peters, with a covering note recommending that he deal with the matter. Soon afterwards the Registrar received another, similar letter, this time from a bookshop in nearby Burford, about an unpaid bill for books and maps. This, too, was forwarded to Peters. After a second letter from the same bookshop, also forwarded, Peters replied to the Registrar, explaining that he had been 'ill and out of action' for about a week. A doctor had deemed that 'the trouble is due to overwork'. This was why he had been unable to post the promised cheque to the bookshop.

A little later, complaints began to arrive from Miss Anne

		Registration District			
1958		Marriage solemnized at			the Regi
	District of		OXFORD		in the
Columns —	1	2	3	4	
No.	When married.	Name and surname.	Age.	Condition.	
113	Twenty second March,	Robert Peters	30 years	Bachelor	
	1958	Marie Alison Hamilton Baillie	22 years	Spinster	
Married in the Register Office					

Certificate of the marriage between Robert Peters and his
fourth wife, Marie Baillie, in 1958. Note that Peters gives his
age as thirty, though in fact he was ten years older.

Dreydel, Principal of St Clare's Hall, in those days a higher education college for young women in North Oxford, where Peters
had been teaching. Trevor-Roper did not enquire into the nature
of these complaints, and Boase did not elaborate, except to say
that Peters had indignantly repudiated them. Attached to one of
them was the original letter from Peters offering his services as a
tutor at St Clare's. He had claimed to possess a first-class degree in
modern history – from Magdalen, taken in 1945. Questioned by
Trevor-Roper about this startling avowal, the President squashed
it. Peters had never been seen at Magdalen until recently.

From this moment on, everything professed by Peters began
to seem suspect. If he claimed a first-class degree at Magdalen,
which was demonstrably false, how could one believe his claim
of a first-class degree at London?

Boase had asked himself the same question. He explained to

Trevor-Roper that he had already made confidential enquiries at London, and found that in 1953 one 'Robert Parkin Peters' had registered as an external student for a BA degree in history. To qualify for the course, Peters had been first required to sit Intermediate Arts examinations – the equivalent of A-levels – in English, Latin and history; he had failed in all three subjects. The Registrar stated quite definitely that no Robert Peters (or Robert Parkin Peters) held a degree from the University of London.

Another disquieting detail was that, in his application to the University of London, Robert Parkin Peters had given his date of birth as 11 August 1918: the same day and the same month, but ten years earlier than the date on his marriage certificate (and six years earlier than on his application to Magdalen). Assuming that he was indeed the same Robert Peters, he was not thirty years old as he had told his wife, or thirty-four as he had told Trevor-Roper, but forty.

This was concerning, but worse was to come. The President fished out another letter, addressed to him some five years before, in 1953. It had come from William Taeusch, Dean of the College of Wooster, Ohio, where a man calling himself Robert Parkin Peters was employed as a lecturer in history. Doubts had arisen there about his credentials. Had he in fact been at Magdalen, the letter enquired, and taken a first-class degree in 1939?

To the people at Wooster, 'Robert Parkin Peters' seemed to have excellent qualifications: as well as his first in history from Magdalen, he claimed to have been awarded a Diploma in Education by Oxford in 1940 and an MA in 1944. His application to Wooster had been supported by two typed letters from Magdalen, one signed by the then President, Boase's predecessor, the eminent scientist Sir Henry Tizard, and another signed by a tutor who had since left the college to take up a post at the Ministry of Labour. ('He is a young man of considerable academic brilliance, who should have a most interesting and successful career.')

Boase himself had dealt with the enquiry from Wooster, though he had evidently forgotten the episode by the time that Peters gained admission to Magdalen four years later. Back in 1953, he had informed Dean Taeusch that there was no record of anybody of that name having been a member of Magdalen. It followed that the testimonial letters, and the signatures, must have been forgeries. In due course he had heard back from Wooster. Another testimonial, this one from the University of Adelaide, had proved to be a forgery. 'Investigation revealed also that Mr Robert Parkin Peters did not have the right credentials for living in this country,' the Dean continued. 'Accordingly last Friday he was taken into custody by officials of the Immigration Bureau who I understand are in the process of deporting him. We at the same time have of course terminated his contract with us.'

The President had written to thank the Dean of Wooster for letting him know the outcome of 'this most curious case'. Given subsequent events, his words were pregnant with irony. Peters was 'obviously a man of striking gifts, who has succeeded in obtaining posts at many distinguished institutions. We are taking what steps we can to make his conduct known over here and I hope he will not again succeed in persuading people of the genuineness of his references.'

TWO

In which the parson is ejected from Oxford

Sitting in his rooms with Trevor-Roper five years later, the President of Magdalen had reason to feel embarrassed. Having learned that someone called 'Robert Parkin Peters' had fraudulently claimed to possess a degree from his college, and having assured the Dean of Wooster that steps were being taken to make his misconduct known to others in Oxford, he had allowed a man with an almost identical name to gain admission to Magdalen, to pass four terms there undisturbed, indeed to hold a wedding ceremony in the college chapel. It was not until complaints began arriving from St Clare's that his suspicions had been aroused.

Consciousness of his earlier negligence quickened his determination now. By the time that Trevor-Roper called on him, Boase had already written to Peters to request that he produce two essential documents: his birth certificate and the certificate of his London degree; and when no immediate answer was forthcoming, he had summoned him to another interview: 'it is essential to clear up this point.' Just possibly the Robert Peters of late 1950s Magdalen was not the Robert Parkin Peters who had claimed to be a pre-war Magdalen alumnus.

Mrs Peters had replied on behalf of her husband, pleading that he was too ill to attend at the time proposed and promising that he would get in touch as soon as he was able. A week later the President had written to Peters again, in still firmer terms: though sorry to hear that his illness continued, he regarded the question of the certificates as a matter that could have been dealt with by post; unless he received a satisfactory response by the end of the following week, 'we shall have to remove your name from the college books'. Once again Mrs Peters had replied, this time at length and in a resentful tone. 'My husband's illness is an organic illness and not, as some malicious people have suggested, a mental condition,' she wrote. She had not shown him the President's letter, she went on, since she had been endeavouring to shield him from all worry. Her own letter displayed her absolute faith in her husband. She referred darkly to 'allegations of an institution in Oxford, the reputation of which in University circles is well-known' – meaning, presumably, St Clare's Hall. 'My husband had reason, some weeks ago, to address a strong letter to that institution because of the false rumours and allegations which he had reason to believe they were making about his character.' She had no doubt that, once recovered, he would insist on a full inquiry, which would utterly exonerate him. Later in the letter she again referred to 'unfounded and malicious rumours which have been set in motion by various people, whose activities we are in the process of tracing and firmly quashing, about the character of my husband and myself'. She hinted at the possibility of legal action. 'May I finally point out,' she wrote, 'what a bitter injustice it is that my husband, who has such a love for the beauty and tradition of Magdalen, should be treated to these indignities.' He had been one of the very few members of the college, she continued, who had thought it worthwhile to attend the service of thanksgiving to mark the 500th anniversary of the college's charter, granted in 1458. 'He has shown his love and respect for the college, to which he is so proud to belong, in every possible way.'

Unimpressed by this emotional appeal, Boase had continued to press Peters for his birth certificate and other evidence of his identity and qualifications. When Mrs Peters protested that her husband was still seriously ill, and unable to see people or write letters, the President asked for a medical certificate. After a delay, a certificate arrived, with an illegible signature.

So the matter stood when Trevor-Roper called on Boase in mid-December 1958. He had come to see the President believing Peters to be a blameless naïf, albeit perhaps a deluded one. As more and more evidence of Peters's untruthfulness emerged from the Magdalen records, it became less and less possible to maintain this view. Under scrutiny, his vivid stories collapsed. Nothing he said could be taken on trust. Was he really being persecuted by the Bishop of Oxford? Had he truly been ordained by Bishop Bayne of Olympia? And so on. At best he was a fantasist; at worst an inveterate liar. Rather than an innocent victim, Peters was beginning to appear a predatory fraud.

It was understandable for Trevor-Roper to feel foolish, and perhaps a little aggrieved, after being taken in so. Though a fine scholar, he was not some unworldly, head-in-the-clouds academic, to be easily gulled: he was a master of deception himself, a code-breaker and intelligence analyst during the war, and a barracuda in the treacherous waters of academic politics. His sympathy for Peters was replaced by harsher feelings. But at the same time his interest was piqued. He enjoyed poking fun at the pompous and the respectable. Exotic and unusual characters drew his interest. As was becoming evident, he was by no means alone in being taken in by Peters: bishops, deans, heads of colleges and professors had been deceived by him. Indeed, Peters's own wife seemingly still believed in him, despite the accumulating evidence against his name. Trevor-Roper marvelled at Peters's plausibility.

Among the documents that President Boase extracted from the file to show Trevor-Roper was the single-sentence testimonial that had accompanied Peters's original application to Magdalen. This stated merely that the writer knew Peters and thought him capable of historical research. At the foot of this typed letter Trevor-Roper recognised the familiar signature of his fellow historian Joel Hurstfield, and it occurred to him to ask Hurstfield how much he knew about the man. Boase readily assented to this proposal, and they parted with an agreement to pool whatever information about Peters they could collect. Accordingly, Trevor-Roper wrote to Hurstfield, referring to the testimonial and asking whether it was genuine: 'Such curious facts are coming to light that I am not prepared to believe any of it unless you positively say that you wrote it.'

In reply, Hurstfield explained that Peters had turned up in London claiming to have a first-class degree from Oxford, and on the strength of this claim had been admitted to the postgraduate seminar in early modern history run jointly by himself and Neale – just as he had later done in Oxford, though he was then claiming a London degree. Indeed, there was a pleasing symmetry about Peters's claims. After only a month or so in London he was gone, 'to take up a tutorial post at Magdalen College, Oxford'. It was just before leaving that he had solicited the bald testimonial from Hurstfield. Sometime afterwards, at the Institute of Historical Research,* Hurstfield had been buttonholed by Peters, who asked for a quarter of an hour of his time. Peters explained that some difficulty had arisen in Oxford about his credentials. The trouble, he said, had been provoked by a jilted admirer of his wife's, who had spread slanders about the couple in Oxford. (In this story Trevor-Roper recognised another version of Peters's account of persecution by the Bishop of Oxford.) Declining to comment, Hurstfield had told Peters firmly that he was not to use his name as a referee in the future, as he had evidently been doing in the recent past, since both he and Neale had received enquiries about Peters from prospective employers. Peters's testimonial had been intended for one purpose only, to support his candidacy for the post at Magdalen.

While Trevor-Roper had been exchanging letters with Hurstfield, Boase was pursuing his own enquiries. Some days after receiving Peters's medical certificate, Boase wrote again to Mrs Peters, which elicited a long letter of bluster from Peters himself, now risen from his sickbed. 'My wife caught quite a severe cold as a result of going to see Dr Mullins [the GP] on a very wet night in order to obtain that certificate,' he wrote accusingly; 'this request has shocked others than ourselves.' Rather than acceding to the President's request, he sought shelter in the intricacy of college procedures: 'If you still feel it necessary, after this full explanation of mine, to take further action in the surprising manner you suggested in your letter of 10 December, I shall

---

* Hurstfield was slightly surprised to encounter him there. As Trevor-Roper would discover, Peters had a habit of lurking in academic institutes, looking busy.

exercise the right, which I understand is mine, of appealing to the Visitor, and, if necessary, to the Chancellor, for his permission to migrate to another college, in order that I may complete, as I ought to be enabled to, my already well-advanced work here.'

Though lacking in certificates, Peters showed a preternatural knowledge of college procedure. He was correct in his understanding that he had the right of appeal to the Visitor, in this case the Bishop of Winchester, who fulfilled the role *ex officio*. A Visitor is an overseer who has the authority to determine disputes arising between the college and its members – though in practice this power is only rarely invoked or exercised.

Boase was not to be deflected, however. He reiterated his request to see the certificates. Peters continued to stall. 'This morning I have received intelligence that within a day or so I ought to receive information which when placed before you ought to bring to an end this distasteful and embarrassing situation in which I have been unjustly placed,' he wrote on 14 January 1959. When the President insisted on another interview, Peters again used illness as an excuse not to come – this time not his own, but his wife's: 'My wife has suffered a nervous collapse as a result of all this unfortunate business.' The President received a letter expressing concern for Mrs Peters from his opposite number, the Principal of Lady Margaret Hall, Lucy Sutherland, historian of the East India Company.

The doctor's certificate had stated that Peters was ill and unable to attend to business. But in fact Peters was attending to his own business. All this time he was writing furiously, about the archdeaconry of St Albans. While he made his apology to the President for being unable to attend an interview, he applied to the history faculty board for leave to submit his thesis two terms ahead of time, so that examiners could be appointed at the board's next meeting on 29 January. His supervisor, Miss Major, objected on intellectual grounds: it would be a better thesis if he took longer over it. But Peters was not persuaded. He had special reasons, he said, for this haste; reasons of a personal, even private nature. It would soon become apparent what these reasons were.

A week or two after his interview with Boase, Trevor-Roper received a telephone call from another Oxford historian, John Owen of Lincoln College. Owen, a New Zealander, had consulted him some six months earlier about a senior lectureship in his native Christchurch; now he reported on developments. An Oxford man had been selected, and his appointment was imminent. Though not very impressive in person, he had excellent qualifications on paper: a first-class degree in theology from Oxford as well as a first-class degree in history from London, and a Ph.D. from Washington. While in London he had edited, for Professor Sir John Neale, the Commons' Journal* in the reign of Elizabeth I. Another point in his favour was that he was married to a New Zealand girl (in fact a former pupil of Owen). Originally he had wanted to postpone taking up his appointment, but now he begged that there should be no delay – on account of his wife's illness.

The New Zealand electors had already informed their chosen candidate that his election was a mere formality. Owen had therefore been disconcerted to receive a letter from a friend at the University of London, urging him to do nothing in the matter without consulting Trevor-Roper. The friend, of course,

---

* The formal record of the business of the House of Commons, day by day. Later, when told of this claim, Neale would dismiss it as 'utterly ridiculous'.

was Joel Hurstfield, and the 'Oxford man' was Robert Peters. 'Good God!' Trevor-Roper exclaimed into the telephone when that fatal name was uttered. He advised Owen to speak at once to Boase, and to cable his compatriots in New Zealand to stay their hand if possible.

Perhaps aware that his past was catching up with him, Peters sought an urgent interview with the chairman of the history faculty board at Oxford, Steven Watson. He was accompanied by his wife, now recovered from her nervous collapse. Peters complained that he was the victim of a campaign of slander, as a result of an alleged offence said to have taken place some years before, the issuing of a false cheque. He feared that these slanders were damaging his career and might be used to prevent his thesis being accepted by the board. One of the slanders was that he beat his wife, which, as the chairman could see, was manifestly untrue. Would he care to examine her for bruises?

Watson responded cautiously. It seemed to him obvious that Peters was dotty – though his wife seemed sane, and yet she played her part seriously in this bizarre comedy. Among the slanders, said Peters, was one directed against his London degree, on which his status in Oxford depended. His college, Magdalen, had either lost the relevant documentation or was concealing it, for reasons unknown. He had been advised, he said, by a well-wisher, the Beit Professor of Colonial History, to keep out of the President of Magdalen's way, which he was doing; and complained further that the Bishop of Oxford had taken against him, as a clergyman of the Old Catholic rite,* on

---

* 'Old Catholic' is an umbrella term to describe sects that have broken away from the Roman Catholic Church over issues of doctrine (mostly

doctrinal grounds. (One can imagine that Bishop Bayne might also have taken against him, had he been aware of this.)

Watson dismissed his fears. Provided that his papers were in order – provided that his college had entered him and his supervisor had signed her approval – the board would carry out its duties and appoint examiners to assess his thesis regardless of any extraneous circumstances.

More evidence, as yet fragmentary and insubstantial, was emerging from the mists of the past. The President of Magdalen had been delving deeper into the college archives: it seemed possible that Peters was a clergyman who had been defrocked for bigamy some years before. The Principal of St Clare's Hall suddenly recalled that as long ago as 1946, while she had been an undergraduate at St Anne's, the university authorities had circulated a warning against accepting a man named Robert Parkin or Parkins. It had yet to be confirmed that this was the same Robert Peters now at Magdalen, or the 'Robert Parkin Peters' who had applied to London. In any case the President refused to allow himself to become diverted from his path. He insisted on seeing the missing documents. When Peters continued to procrastinate, Boase presented him with an ultimatum: produce the certificates, or your name will be struck off the books of the college. On 28 January Peters dispatched a letter to Boase explaining that he was 'laid up' and enclosing another medical certificate. But it was too late: that very day a line in red ink was drawn through Peters's name in the college roll. At a stroke of the pen he ceased to be a member of Magdalen.

---

concerning papal authority). Some Old Catholic churches are in communion with the Church of England.

Boase informed Peters's supervisor and the university authorities of what had happened. He also took the precaution of writing to the Visitor, alerting him that he might receive an appeal from Peters. 'I have not heard from Mr Robert Peters and I shall now be forewarned,' replied the bishop, the Right Reverend Alwyn Williams. 'I have however heard of him in the ecclesiastical field and know that there is much past history!'

The next day the faculty board met. When the name of Peters came up, it was explained that he was no longer a member of his college and therefore that his application had lapsed. No examiners were appointed.

That same afternoon, Peters – though still, according to his medical certificate, too ill to deal with correspondence – was entertaining a reluctant John Owen to tea, and feeding him a tale of misfortune, interspersed with some violent language, in which two villains loomed large, the President of Magdalen and the Regius Professor of Modern History. This pair, Peters said, had been the architects of his ruin. Ostensibly his ruin had been caused by a lack of documents; but in fact there was a perfectly rational explanation for that unfortunate lack, which had been cruelly exploited by his enemies. He had submitted a certificate of his first-class honours degree from London at the time of his application to Magdalen. The President, with culpable negligence, had lost the document, and was now demanding a replacement. But in fact this was impossible. For the University of London had a statute whereby any graduate who was convicted of a criminal offence was automatically struck out of the register, as if he (or she) had never been. Unfortunately, in 1950 Peters had been convicted of such an offence – issuing a false cheque* – and so, although there was no doubting the fact of his degree, all evidence of it had been totally and finally expunged from the university records. The only surviving evidence was Peters's own certificate, and that certificate, now irreplaceable, had been lost ...

What was he to do in such a predicament? As the President's letters had become more menacing (so he told Owen), he had sought counsel from a friend at Keble, Douglas Price (another historian of Elizabethan England, not a natural ally of the Regius Professor), who had drawn in the college's law tutor and Bursar, Vere Davidge. The two had been firm and unanimous in their advice. The President of Magdalen, they said, is well known throughout the university as a crook: nothing but harm can come of seeing him. Therefore Peters must work against time, hasten to complete his thesis for examination at the earliest opportunity, ready himself to leave for the other side of the world – and on no account see Boase. Silence, evasion, pretended illness: all means were fair to keep the President at bay until his thesis was finished, submitted, examined and passed, and Robert Peters, B.Litt., was on his way to New Zealand. This, so he said, was the strong, united advice of the Fellows of Keble. And though the President seemed to have forestalled him, Peters refused to accept defeat. Against Tom Boase, as President of Magdalen, he would appeal to the Visitor; and against Tom Boase, as Vice-Chancellor, he would appeal to the Chancellor.

(Later, when told of this story, Davidge would write to Boase

---

* Like so many of Peters's stories, this one had a kernel of truth. He had been convicted of issuing a false cheque, though not in 1950, and his name had not been expunged from any register as a result.

to assure him that he had never given legal advice to Peters: 'I do not even know the man, but I am told he once dined here as somebody else's guest on a night when I was dining.')

According to Peters, the campaign against him originated in slurs spread by another New Zealand woman in Oxford whom his wife had unwisely befriended, who had turned against her and had spread spiteful gossip about unhappy marital relations, wife-beating, etc. Such slanders (which of course were unfounded) had reached the ears of the Principal of St Clare's Hall, the Bishop of Oxford and others. Though the details differed, there were obvious similarities between the account Peters had given to Owen and those he had given to Watson, Hurstfield and Trevor-Roper. Each was a device to cover his tracks, and to divert, or at least to delay, his pursuer, the President of Magdalen. By this time Peters had told so many different stories about himself that (one imagines) he must have found it difficult to keep track of what he had said to whom. It seems surprising that Mrs Peters maintained her belief in him so long.

Owen was conscious that much if not all of what he was being told was fabricated, but he gave Peters a hearing out of a very serious concern for his wife. He made no indication to Peters that he had spoken to either the Regius Professor or the President of Magdalen. He had already decided to recommend to the electors of Christchurch that they should withdraw their offer.

This tea party chez Peters took place on 29 January 1959. Meanwhile there had been developments elsewhere. Trevor-Roper had imprudently told his wife the unusual tale of Robert Peters, and soon afterwards Lady Alexandra, not known for her discretion, had imprudently related it to her hosts at the breakfast table, while she happened to be staying with the

Regius Professor of Hebrew, Cuthbert Simpson, and his wife. 'But I know this man!' exclaimed Simpson. More than ten years earlier, in his native Canada, he had been in Toronto when a priest calling himself Robert Parkin Peters had been exposed as a fraud. There had been much talk about it at the time, with some publicity. Indeed, if he remembered aright, there had been a succession of scandals attached to Peters's name – that he had been a bigamist, and had been defrocked in England before leaving for Canada and being re-ordained there.* Simpson was appalled at the prospect of such a man in Oxford. 'I will have that man put in prison,' he declared, when he dined with Trevor-Roper on 31 January, a Saturday. Simpson dispatched a letter to a colleague in Canada, to check that Peters was indeed the same scoundrel who had crossed his path more than a decade before. Little did he know then that he would very soon meet him again.

The very next day, a Sunday, Simpson was due to officiate at morning service at the Church of St Mary Magdalen, at the bottom of St Giles', opposite the Randolph Hotel. On Simpson's arrival the incumbent, the Reverend Colin Stevenson, introduced his new assistant, clothed in full vestments: Robert Peters. 'I want a word with you,' a tight-lipped Simpson told the startled vicar, and led him through to the vestry, where he demanded that Stevenson telephone the bishop forthwith. After an episcopal eruption, a shaken Stevenson had no option but to inform Peters that he was no longer welcome at St Mary Magdalen.

By this time the tale of Robert Peters was becoming widely known within the university. Now that he had been rumbled, he had no further motive to remain in Oxford; and, since the net

---

* In fact Simpson had misremembered the sequence of events.

was closing around him, he had an obvious motive to leave, to try his impostures in virgin fields. The Regius Professor decided that the time had come to alert the police. In an interview with the Chief Constable, he recommended investigating Peters as a suspected bigamist and forger, who had impersonated a clergyman, and obtained work under false pretences.

The police commenced enquiries, but found that Peters had fled before they could interview him. He had left Oxford with his wife, after informing Miss Major that they were off to spend a fortnight with some friends of Mrs Peters in Derbyshire.

He did not return after a fortnight; but that was not quite his last bow in Oxford. In mid-February the Registrar of the university received a letter from the Clerk of Hertfordshire County Council. A 'Mr Robert Peters' had applied for a position as assistant archivist. On his application form he stated that he was thirty-one years of age. He claimed to have a first-class degree in history from Oxford, as well as a degree from London. He did not specify his college. The Registrar regretfully informed the county council that he had no record of anyone of that name holding a degree from Oxford (let alone a first-class degree).

Almost eighteen months later, the President of Magdalen would receive a letter from an officer of the Inland Revenue. Letters addressed to Mr Peters, understood to be a research student at Magdalen, had been returned undelivered. Might the college have a current address for him? In his reply, Boase explained that Peters's name had been expunged from the college books in January 1959. 'There is a very long history attached to this case,' the President continued. 'It is most unlikely that we shall at any time have an address for him, and I fear that you will find him a very elusive character.'

PART II

1959–83

THREE

In which the professor studies the parson's past

Two weeks after Peters's flight the story broke. For the press, it offered at least two juicy aspects: a wayward clergyman and the embarrassment of the authorities. 'PETERS THE PARSON HOAXES OXFORD' was a front-page headline in the *Daily Express*. There was even a story in the South African *Cape Times*. Like several other newspapers, the *Cape Times* quoted an unnamed don as saying of Peters's thesis that it was 'a brilliant piece of work'. The press preferred to depict Peters as an outstanding scholar who had gone to the bad, rather than the reality: that he was at best a mediocre student.

Press coverage of Peters's exploits in Oxford was not censorious. No newspaper at the time referred to him as a liar or a cheat. He was depicted as a hoaxer, a cheeky chappie who might have bent the rules but had done no significant harm. He might even have done some good, in pricking the pomposity of professors, bishops and vice-chancellors. The story could be told as one of the individual against the Establishment, David against Goliath, the nimble Peters running rings around the ponderous dinosaurs of the University of Oxford and the Church of England. Forgery was a victimless crime. It was all a bit of fun.

That, at any rate, was how the press portrayed it at the time. For

POLICE START AN INVESTIGATION

Peters the parson hoaxes Oxford

By SEAMUS BRADY

POLICE are investigating the case of the twice-jailed parson who hoaxed Oxford University into giving him a big social wedding — and almost into giving him a degree.

In Magdalen College last night the conversation was of the chubby-faced Rev. Robert Peters and his exploits during the past 18 months.

For Peters, four times married—once bigamously—has now disappeared from Oxford with his young wife of 11 months.

THE REV. ROBERT
Twice married, twice divorced.
...torate of an American university.

Recommended

Peters had, in fact, been admitted as a candidate for a degree in London, and had become known to one of the historians there.

He said that, on reflection, he would rather come to Oxford, and he persuaded the historian in London to recommend him to an historian in Oxford, who interviewed him, decided he was a competent student and recommended him for admission to Magdalen College as a candidate for a Bachelor of Letters degree.

At Magdalen, when he was interviewed, Peters was asked about his documents, and said they were with another university to which he had applied

Student

He was admitted to the college as a research student after claiming to hold a first-class honours degree in history from London University, a doctorate in philosophy from America, and a degree in theology from Oxford.

What the authorities did not know was that he was Robert Parkins Peters, ordained a Church of England priest at Wakefield in 1941, but later unfrocked.

In 1946 he failed to surrender to his bail on a bigamy charge at Fort William, in Scotland. He went to Australia, later to Canada. In the United States he became a college lecturer.

Cutting from the front page of the *Daily Express*, 27 February 1959.
Internal evidence suggests that Trevor-Roper was a source.

those who had been duped it was more serious. For the Bishop of Oxford it was disturbing to discover that an unfrocked priest had officiated at services in his diocese. It transpired that Peters had been connected with St Mary Magdalen for some weeks before being unmasked, despite the 'illness' that had prevented him from attending several summonses from the President of Magdalen. He had officiated at a number of weddings, rendering these unlawful. This was an uncomfortable discovery for all concerned.

It was unsettling, too, for the university authorities. The whole hierarchy of higher education, from the selection of candidates for admission as undergraduates to the appointment of professors, was founded on a system of accreditation, attested to by certificates and testimonials; if these could not be relied upon, the implications were alarming. By the time he came to Trevor-Roper's attention, Peters was already adept at forgery. One of his tactics was to inveigle his way into an institution and then purloin some of its headed paper, on which he could write his own references. Sometimes these would end in a scrawled signature, but more often he would produce an unsigned 'copy' of the so-called original. In support of his application to Magdalen, for example, Peters had attached a handwritten testimonial on headed paper from Miss K. M. Hobbs, Principal of a firm of private tutors. He had been a full-time tutor on her staff, it said, and she had formed the impression that he would make excellent use of his time as a research student at Oxford. No one seems to have noticed the similarity between the hand in which it was penned and the hand in which the application itself had been written.

It was troubling, too, that Peters was a student of history. Forgery is particularly problematic for historians. Documents are the building blocks from which a historical work is constructed; their authenticity provides its structural strength. The whiff of forgery is like the smell of dry rot, threatening to bring the whole edifice crashing down.

The Regius Professor was a stern critic of historians whose scholarship he felt to be wanting. He was especially harsh on what he saw as intellectual dishonesty. Some years earlier he had published a pitiless assault on the work of a former pupil, Lawrence Stone, which caused certain historians to think him unbalanced. 'What this whole business goes to show,' his predecessor as Regius Professor of Modern History, the medievalist V. H. Galbraith, had remarked, 'is that Stone is no scholar and Trevor-Roper is no gentleman.' Trevor-Roper was a prickly colleague, tenacious in his insistence on rigour, even when others might have thought it better to let the matter drop. For him, however, this was the duty of the historian. History was not a game; it was the foundation of everything worthwhile. Truth needed to be defended from ideological bias, from sloppy scholarship and from lies. Men like Peters had to be kept out of the profession. The fact that Trevor-Roper had chosen to involve the police shows how seriously he took Peters's impostures.

But though severe, Trevor-Roper was not solemn. He had a keen sense of the ridiculous, evident in his hesitant delivery, which suggested a man perpetually on the edge of a chuckle, amused by the absurdities that he identified around him. He was fascinated by the limitless credulity of the human mind. He saw the world as governed, and its horizons limited, by people and institutions who took its appearances and conventions for granted, and who were too lazy or cowardly or unimaginative to think outside them. Characters like Peters provided a splash of colour in an otherwise grey world.

This, perhaps, was the reason why the professor chose to pursue Peters after he had fled Oxford. There was no onus on him to do anything further once the reprobate had disappeared over the horizon. Nevertheless, Trevor-Roper took it upon himself to instigate an inquiry into the parson's past. If the police would not act, he would play detective. He opened a dossier on Peters, which would grow thicker over the years as he accumulated documents from informants across the globe. Periodically he would receive fresh word of 'our old friend', as Peters applied for posts in Wisconsin, Ottawa, Washington, Illinois, Dublin, Kuala Lumpur and elsewhere. It was not always easy to establish the facts about Peters, given that the personal details he provided varied from occasion to occasion. Peters appeared in a bewildering array of guises, sometimes emerging into view close to home, sometimes far away. But though the guises were different, the tactics were the same: assume a position based on forged qualifications, maintain a lofty superiority, aggressively repel challenges until continuing becomes impossible, and then flee.

In the week following Peters's flight from Oxford, Trevor-Roper dispatched a number of letters seeking confidential information about him. It quickly became apparent that 'Parson Peters' was a familiar name in Fleet Street. *The Sunday Times*, to which Trevor-Roper was a regular contributor, obligingly provided copies of their cuttings on the 'Romeo Rev'.

'Shall I keep you up to date in the matter of Robert Peters?' wrote Trevor-Roper to Joel Hurstfield. 'Depth is now opening on depth and ever new and more fantastic revelations are coming out of them.' He outlined what he had discovered so far of Peters's past. In 1947, a schoolmaster awaiting trial on a charge of bigamy, Peters had jumped bail and fled the country. He had taken refuge

Parson accused of bigamy
(arrest ordered in Scotland) is in Switzerland

THE Rev. Robert Michael Parkins, spectacled, twenty-eight-year-old Church of England parson for whom Fort William (Inverness-shire) police yesterday issued an arrest warrant after he had failed to surrender to his bail on a charge of bigamy, was in Switzerland last night.

From an expensive hotel on the banks of Lake Geneva he told the *Daily Mirror* no one had advised him of the date when he was required to surrender to his bail.

"This is terrible; it is all a ghastly mistake," he said.

Beside him as he spoke over

Mr. Parkins. Miss Gladdish

the phone to London was Margaret Wright Gladdish, the pretty nurse from the Children's Hospital, Great Ormond-street, London, whom he is alleged to have married "while

being the lawful husband of Hilda Mary Brunton."

When Mr. Parkins appeared before the Fort William Sheriff Court six weeks ago on the bigamy charge he was allowed £20 bail.

The Scottish Crown Office decided the case should be dealt with by the Fort William Court.

Yesterday, when the name "Robert Michael Parkins" was called there was no answer, and Sheriff Cameron Miller ordered a warrant for his arrest.

Mr. James Thompson, solicitor for the defence, said as his client had failed to appear he would no longer act on his behalf.

Scotland Yard was immediately informed, and inquiries were begun in Warrington, Lancs, where the woman said to be his lawful wife lives.

Cutting from the front page of the *Daily Mirror*, 8 January 1947.

in a hotel on Lake Geneva. He told a press reporter who caught up with him there that he was making arrangements to return to England at the earliest possible moment, insisting that he had nothing to fear from the charge, 'the whole thing being false'. Peters had been rearrested while staying in a mountain resort under the name 'Mr Humphreys'.* He had been deported and placed on the Paris express *en route* to England; but he had left the train as it passed through France, and had made his way to Marseilles, where he had boarded a ship bound for the East. He

---

* He was said to have been arrested at gunpoint for failing to pay his hotel bill (almost a capital offence in Switzerland).

was briefly Principal of the Anglican Divinity School in Ceylon.* His application for this post had come in the form of a telegram, which had arrived after the Bishop had left for England, and had been closely followed by Peters himself, who had established himself in the Bishop's Palace and had taken over the school. The Diocesan Secretary had sent a report to the Bishop praising his work. His Grace had boasted of his successful appointment in his London club, where one of his auditors, recognising Peters from the description, had informed the startled Bishop that his efficient new assistant was wanted by the police. It became apparent that he had forged the references supporting his application and claimed degrees that he did not hold. Arrangements were made for his repatriation; but rather than taking ship back to England, Peters had headed in the opposite direction, to Singapore, and then to Australia, where he taught in a school. At some point he had abandoned his second wife on a train. He had obtained teaching posts at colleges in Canada and the United States – the last being at the College of Wooster, Ohio – before being arrested by the FBI and deported in 1953. And so on. Everywhere he went, so it seemed, he had left a trail of forged documents, deserted women and unpaid bills.

'You will see from all this that he is a man of infinite intellectual resources,' wrote the Regius Professor in his letter to

---

* 'The Rev. Robert Parkins M.A. (Oxon.) has arrived from Europe to be the new Principal of the Divinity School, when it reopens in July,' reported the *Ceylon Churchman* in its May 1947 issue. 'Fr. Parkins was at Magdalen College, Oxford, and is described as "a most able teacher, a real scholar, and an expert in his line, Theology" ... We welcome him and Mrs Parkins, and feel that they will be a valuable asset to our Diocesan life.'

Hurstfield. 'Every day brings in new evidence of this fact.' Though he thought it desirable to expose Peters as a liar, he asked Hurstfield to keep the contents of the letter to himself, given that Peters 'is extremely litigious, and is spreading scandalous stories about everyone (including myself) about Oxford'. This, Trevor-Roper would find, was a characteristic ploy: whenever Peters felt in danger of being unmasked, he would counter-attack, seeking to discredit his accuser or accusers with slander and innuendo, and threatening legal action. He would never retract, or apologise; he appeared to have no shame, and therefore no conscience. An egotist, he was indifferent to the thoughts and feelings of those whom his actions might have damaged; other people, it seemed, existed solely to serve his purposes.

Hurstfield was similarly fascinated by the revelations about Peters. 'Surely the thing will be published one day! It will make far more interesting reading than *The Quest for Corvo*.'* Hurstfield was especially interested to learn that Peters had been in a hurry to present his thesis to the Oxford history faculty board. He recalled that during the previous summer Peters had borrowed a Ph.D. thesis by another of his students on a similar topic. Several letters had failed to secure the return of the thesis, and only after a good many months did it come back, without any note or comment of any kind. Hurstfield thought

---

* A. J. A. Symons's *The Quest for Corvo* (1934) was a life of the eccentric author, artist, photographer and fraud Frederick Rolfe, who used the pseudonym Baron Corvo. Subtitled 'An Experiment in Biography', the book told the story of the author's investigation of his subject, presenting aspects of Rolfe's life and character as they were revealed to him. Trevor-Roper would liken his own 'quest for Backhouse' to the quest for Corvo.

it possible that Peters's thesis owed 'not a little' to this other student's work.

'As the story unfolds the humorous side gives place to one of alarm as one contemplates the damage he has done and can do,' observed Hurstfield. 'It must be extraordinarily difficult to stop a man like this in his tracks, but it looks as though he is going to be active in academic circles for some time, and some of our vulnerable colleagues might need to be forewarned.' In a correspondence stretching over several letters, Hurstfield and Trevor-Roper discussed what might be done to halt Peters, or at least to handicap him. Trevor-Roper considered publishing a warning against Peters in the *Times Educational Supplement*; but he was concerned that this might provoke an action for libel, and in such an eventuality he was not convinced that *The Times* would pay the costs of defending an action. (Trevor-Roper had enough experience of libel suits to make him wary.) The two men discussed whether there might be a case for a criminal prosecution. Both agreed to collect evidence: 'the important thing, of course, is [to obtain] documents in the scoundrel's own hand.' Hurstfield hoped that sooner or later Peters would supply sufficient evidence in writing 'to enable us to lay him by the heels'. He guessed that Peters would soon start plaguing universities with a fresh set of bogus qualifications. 'Do you think they might be interested in him at Reading University?' he asked mischievously.

Trevor-Roper obtained a photocopy of Peters's New Zealand application from the Association of Universities of the British Commonwealth, which served as a clearing house for overseas academic appointments. Its Secretary, Dr J. F. Foster, was 'shaken' to find that Peters had misrepresented his qualifications, especially since he thought it 'not unlikely that this man will come back into our view on some other occasion' – in fact, Foster continued, 'he has, I find, called at this office in the last few days in order to obtain particulars of academic vacancies in other universities.'

Peters's application form gave the Regius Professor much amusement, replete as it was with the clichés recognisable to those familiar with the genre ('the documents are extensive and offer scope for considerable further research in this neglected field'). He particularly enjoyed the title of Peters's putative Ph.D. from the University of Washington, 'the influence of Bede on Alcuin', which seemed to him 'a wonderful parody of a typical B.Litt. thesis!' Trevor-Roper was scornful of what he saw as the pointless hair-splitting so beloved by medieval historians, which he described as 'nuns knitting'. As he pointed out to Hurstfield, the form was also an incriminating document, since it advanced a number of claims that were demonstrably untrue. For example, Peters had attached a copy of a testimonial from the College of Wooster, supposedly signed by the Dean, asserting that he had been employed there during a period when in reality he was languishing in an English prison (of which more later). This, and the other two testimonials (on unheaded paper) attached to the application, were obvious forgeries: in reality, a form of idealised autobiography ('Mr Peters is a man with a deep sense of vocation ... He has a pleasant personality and appears to be a man of very considerable ability ... Mr Peters has a fine mind ... He showed himself to be a man of real scholarship.')

Peters had entered his date of birth as 11 August 1927 on the application form. Thus on three different forms seen by Trevor-Roper, Peters had given three different years of birth: 1928, 1927 and 1918. (On another application which Trevor-Roper saw not

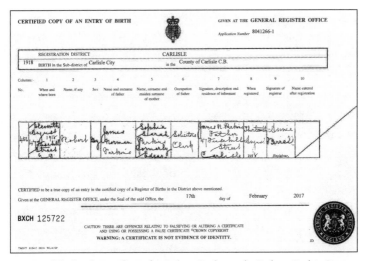

A copy of the birth certificate for Robert Parkins, aka Robert Parkin Peters.

long afterwards, Peters stated that he was born in 1924.) On these forms he had claimed to have degrees in modern history or theology (almost always first class), from either Oxford or London (and sometimes both), in years ranging from 1939 to 1956.

On the same application form Peters claimed to have studied for the priesthood at St Aidan's Theological College in Birkenhead. In response to an enquiry from Trevor-Roper, the Acting Principal of St Aidan's confirmed that Peters had indeed been a student there from 1937 to 1941, and supplied details of his early life that proved accurate. Peters had been born Robert Michael Parkins on 11 August 1918, in Carlisle. His father was not, as he would often suggest, a local solicitor, but a solicitor's clerk. He had been educated at the local grammar school – a Church of England school with strong links to Carlisle Cathedral. As a St Aidan's student he might in normal circumstances have spent a year in Durham (at St John's or St Chad's College) to complete a degree, but it seems that this arrangement was suspended at the outbreak of war in 1939; Peters did not go on to Durham, as might have been expected, though he would later claim that he had done. This disappointment may help to explain his lasting sense of grievance, though it seems a small sacrifice to have made at a time when others of his generation were risking their lives in the national struggle against the Nazi enemy. In 1941 he had been ordained deacon by the Bishop of Wakefield. His first clerical post had been as assistant curate at All Hallows, Almondbury, a village near Huddersfield in West Yorkshire. In 1942 he had been ordained priest, and during 1943–4 he had served as assistant curate at St Mary's, Somers Town, close to Euston Station in London. In 1944 his bishop had withdrawn his licence,* and had made arrangements for him to serve a period of probation. (Technically he was not defrocked but 'inhibited'.) The Acting Principal did not say, and perhaps he did not know, why Peters's licence had been withdrawn; but in view of his subsequent record it is worth noting that his duties as assistant curate included teaching religious education in a girls' school. The Acting Principal saw no reason to suppose that Peters had ever held a bishop's licence since. He quoted from his predecessor as Principal, in fielding an enquiry from a prospective employer: 'I am afraid the college records show that this man has a long record of masquerading as a graduate of various universities.'

---

* Anglican clergy are generally licensed to preach and administer sacraments by the bishop of the diocese(s) in question. However, if a bishop suspends this licence, the deacon or priest may no longer exercise their respective ministerial functions lawfully in that diocese.

Robert Parkins as a student at St Aidan's, Birkenhead, in the late 1930s.

Trevor-Roper was unable to ascertain how Peters had spent the last year of the war, but the gaps in his chronology can be filled from another dossier, kept by Gavin White, a priest outraged by his antics. Expelled from St Mary's, Somers Town, in 1944, Peters began working for the Church Army, an evangelical organisation within the Anglican Communion, and took up residence at the Toc H Christian hostel in Fitzroy Square, London – where he was nicknamed 'Boom Bagshaw', after the preposterous priest* in A. S. M. Hutchinson's bestselling novel (later adapted as a film, then a play, then another film), *If Winter Comes*. He would be asked to leave the hostel when discovered sharing his room with

---

* The Reverend Cyril Boom Bagshaw, a flamboyant character, an actor manqué. A schoolboy who was taught by Parkins in the mid-1940s later recalled him as 'a man of small stature, [with] piercing blue eyes behind heavy dark-rimmed spectacles, booming voice and colossal nerve.'

another man, a clairvoyant who lectured on ghosts – not the kind of person thought desirable in a Christian community.

In the spring of 1945 Peters (still known as Parkins) had commenced his career as a schoolmaster at Lord Weymouth's Grammar School in Warminster, Wiltshire, where he also served as chaplain and took the part of Bottom in a school production of *A Midsummer Night's Dream*.* At the end of the first term he eloped with the deputy headmaster's sister-in-law.

As an inhibited priest Peters was of course forbidden from exercising his ministerial functions, but he seemed unable to resist the urge to do so, even though this risked further episcopal discipline. On Saturday 8 September 1945 a notice in *The Times* reveals that 'the Rev. R. Parkins' would be taking evensong the following day in the chapel of the parish church of St Alban the Martyr, Baldwin Gardens, Holborn. Four months later, on Saturday 12 January 1946, another notice in *The Times* advertised that 'the Rev. R. Parkins of All Saints [*sic*], Almondbury, Huddersfield' would be taking the 6.30 p.m. service on Sunday, in St Paul's Cathedral itself. For an inhibited priest to officiate in such a prominent place seems reckless indeed – though at least Parkins seems to have taken the precaution not to mention his more recent stint as assistant curate of nearby St Mary's, Somers Town.

While Trevor-Roper had been conferring with Hurstfield, Cuthbert Simpson had received a reply from a friend and former colleague, the Reverend Eugene Rathbone Fairweather of Trinity College, Toronto. 'It looks as if you might well have our old pal on your hands,' wrote Fairweather, who, like Simpson

---

* See Gavin Mortimer, *Through the Wren Door – the History of Warminster School* (2019).

himself, had come across Peters as a colleague at Trinity College eleven years earlier, in 1948. 'The name here was "Robert Parkin Peters", and the name under which he had been ordained in England was "Robert Parkins" ... Hence the difficulty of finding him in *Crockford.*'

Crockford's Clerical Directory is a *Who's Who* for the Anglican clergy. As 'Parkins, Robert', Peters had been listed in the 1947 and 1948 issues of *Crockford*; by the 1949–50 issue he had mutated into 'Peters, Robert Parkin'.* By assuming another name, similar to but different from the one he had gone under before, he had presumably hoped to make a new start. 'Peters, Robert Parkin' was listed in one more issue of *Crockford* (1951–2); but by the next (1953–4) he had disappeared, and would not be listed there again.

To assist in Peters's identification Fairweather added a description of the man he remembered:

He was slightly stooped and did not walk easily, because of some old back ailment. It was said that he was more of a cripple than he appeared, and that, for example, he could not reach his shoelaces to tie them. He had a cheerful, round face and a confident manner, an accent that was convincing enough, and a fund of Oxford gossip.

A student who had known Peters in Toronto described him

---

* There was another 'Peters, R. P.' in *Crockford*, one Richard Paul Peters, an apparently blameless character of approximately the same age. He had been ordained in 1939 and was vicar of St Mary's, Easebourne, in the diocese of Chichester, from 1944. In adopting the alias 'Robert Parkin Peters', Robert Parkins may have hoped to exploit any potential confusion between the two, since Anglican priests are often referred to by their initials.

as 'a little man* with a stiff back who walked like a penguin'. His discourse was bombastic and delivered in a loud voice that discouraged interruption.

By this time Trevor-Roper was becoming familiar with Peters's *modus operandi*. His methods were recognisable, even if his motives remained obscure. It was obvious that, though unscrupulous, he was not merely venal; he seemed to crave status rather than riches. Some of his actions were hard to explain in rational terms. He put energy and effort into deceptions that might more profitably have been spent on honest endeavour. He must have realised that few of these deceptions were sustainable; sooner or later he would be found out. But he was a fantasist whose reality was defined by his own imagination. His lies carried so much conviction because he believed them himself. As Trevor-Roper came to appreciate, fantasists are not always rational. Rather than adapting to the world as it is, they attempt to adjust the world to become as they would want it to be.

Within weeks of Peters's hasty departure from Oxford, Trevor-Roper had learned enough of his story to write a three-page summary. It was a complex tale, with more twists and turns than any whodunnit, made more complex still with each new detail. He compiled a curriculum vitae for Peters, which he would repeatedly revise as fresh information arrived in the months and years to follow, as he tracked his quarry from place to place and from country to country. This could then be compared with Peters's own curricula vitae, no two of which were the same, as these trickled into Trevor-Roper's hands from sources around the world.

---

* Peters admitted to being five feet four inches tall.

FOUR

In which the parson pledges to do better

A further search in the Magdalen archives turned up earlier traces of 'Robert Parkins'. In 1946 the High Master of St Paul's School had written a letter of enquiry to Boase's predecessor, Sir Henry Tizard. Somebody called Robert Parkins had applied for a post as a master at St Paul's, claiming to have a first-class degree in modern history from Magdalen: could Sir Henry confirm this claim? In support of his application Parkins had enclosed three glowing testimonials (albeit on unheaded paper): one from the vicar of St Stephen's, Carlisle ('he is beyond doubt a young man of outstanding ability'), another from the Director of Music at Gresham's School in Norfolk, and a third from Gresham's headmaster. This last was an especially skilful piece of headmasterese. 'He has thrown himself wholeheartedly into all aspects of the school's life,' it read. 'He is a most able teacher, a real scholar, and expert in his lines, English and theology. His influence on the boys has been of the best, and he has never satisfied himself, when talking to them, with empty religious sentiments, but has been at great pains to instruct them with no little depth.' As well as being 'an amusing and interesting companion', this paragon was 'quite tireless in all kinds of outside work. He has given up all his spare time to help the clergy of the district, and on some Sundays he has taken six or seven services a day without remuneration in order to help the local parishes where the Vicar has been ill or short-handed.' An unusual further commendation was that Parkins had taken an interest in the diocese of Gambia.*

Tizard knew that no Robert Parkins had been at Magdalen. As soon as he received the enquiry from the High Master of St Paul's, he had written by registered post to the then headmaster of Gresham's, M. J. Olivier (a cousin of the actor Laurence Olivier): 'Can you very kindly tell me whether Mr Parkins represented himself as a member of Magdalen College when he obtained a temporary post at Gresham's School in 1945?'

Olivier's reply had described Parkins's case as 'tragic'. He had applied for a post as assistant master teaching history and divinity at Gresham's in April 1945 – a time when, wrote Olivier, 'I was absolutely desperate for men'. He had offered Parkins the post, commencing in the autumn term, 'as I would have done to almost anybody who had not got a criminal record or proven insanity'. As Parkins's application had said nothing about a degree, Olivier had assumed that he was 'not a Varsity man'. After he had been at Gresham's a while, however, Parkins had bashfully revealed that he had an MA from Oxford – not from Magdalen, but from Keble. Then another master had arrived at the school who himself had been at Keble, and a brief conversation between the

---

* Its full title was the diocese of Gambia and the Rio Pongas. According to the Bishop of Gambia and the Rio Pongas, Parkins/Peters had tried to take control of the Gambia Association, but was regarded as suspect and had failed to make headway.

two had been enough to make it obvious that Parkins had never been a student there. Soon after Parkins had left, for reasons Olivier did not specify. He had provided Parkins with a testimonial, though not, it seems, the one submitted to St Paul's. His own had been more cautiously phrased; indeed, since Parkins's departure, Olivier had told Tizard, he had been 'more and more overwhelmed by requests from other headmasters for an amplification of my testimonial'. The tragedy was that Parkins had proved to be 'a very good and efficient master':

> He has this mania for giving himself a degree, and there are no limits to which he will not go to try to convince people that he has one. It used to be a third in theology at Keble. It is now a first in history at Magdalen. I expect it will soon be a Fellowship at All Souls.

M. J. Olivier's successor as Gresham's headmaster, Logie Bruce Lockhart,* would be more forthcoming about the reasons for Parkins's sudden departure. In a telephone conversation, he told Trevor-Roper that Parkins had disappeared from Gresham's after a colleague, Major Kerridge, who ran the school OTC, had complained of his 'unwanted and improper advances' towards his daughter. There was also a rumour that he had driven boys around the locality in a baby Austin to collect money, supposedly for local charities, which he had pocketed for himself.

From Gresham's Parkins had headed north, to take up a post

---

* A former Scotland fly half, whose father and brother were both also headmasters of public schools.

as Rector of St Columba's Episcopal Church, Grantown-on-Spey, in the Scottish Highlands – though how he was able to do this without a bishop's licence is unknown. A little later a story reached Gresham's that Parkins had extorted a very large sum of money, rumoured to be in the region of £2,000,* from a pair of old ladies at a fishing hotel in the Highlands.

In August 1946, at St Andrew's Episcopal Church in Fort William, Parkins married Miss Margaret Gladdish, a twenty-two-year-old nurse from London, whom he may have met in 1944, while serving as a volunteer fire-watcher at University College Hospital. She had not accompanied him on his travels since, but perhaps they had kept in touch by correspondence. Now the lovers were together at last, united in a sacred bond. But it quickly became known that there was an impediment: Parkins was still legally bound to an earlier wife, formerly Miss Hilda Brunton, a schoolmistress from Warrington, whom he had married three years earlier, in 1943. Parkins was arrested, charged with bigamy† and released on bail. It was then that, forfeiting his bail of £20, he had fled abroad on a whirlwind tour that (as Trevor-Roper had told Joel Hurstfield) had taken him around the world, via Switzerland (where he had served as chaplain in the Anglican church of Lausanne), France, Malta, Egypt, India, Ceylon, Singapore, Australia, and possibly other

---

* The equivalent of more than £70,000 today.

† A serious crime. On 15 October 1947, for example, the Reverend Charles Lamb received a sentence of eighteen months' imprisonment with hard labour after being convicted of bigamy. And in 2008 Roderick Sangster, a former police officer and Church of Scotland minister, was jailed for three years after he was convicted of bigamy and forgery.

places, too, never staying anywhere longer than a few months. He applied for admission to the General Theological Seminary in New York, but was refused an entry visa by the US authorities. While a temporary teacher (for one term only) at St Peters's College, a school in South Australia, he had contrived to receive an MA (*ad eundem*) from the University of Adelaide, where he was lecturing in the Department of Adult Education. This was, of course, on the basis of his claim to be an MA Oxon. An *ad eundem* degree is a courtesy or honorary title granted by one college or university to an alumnus of another.

He appears to have been in a hurry to leave Australia, implying in letters to the Provost of Trinity College (part of the University of Toronto) that he would accept any kind of post even if the stipend were low, and even suggesting that he would be willing to travel to Canada without a firm offer of employment. Asked how he could be in a position to leave his teaching post in Australia in mid-term, he provided an unconvincing excuse. But on the strength of his claim to have a first in theology from Magdalen, and the usual impressive testimonial, he was taken on to the staff of Trinity as a lay theologian. Once there, Parkins rapidly made himself unpopular by his haughty manner towards students and other inferiors ('Sir, I do not think that I know you'), which gave widespread offence, even in an era when Englishmen felt able to be routinely condescending towards Canadians. Gavin White, then an arts student in his final year of study, assumed that all Englishmen were like Parkins; later, relieved to discover otherwise, he would conclude that much of Parkins/Peters's success in convincing people of his bona fides depended on his rudeness. 'He was not pleasant in personal relationships,' White would write:

He would work himself into a position of authority and then use that position to put people down. And nothing he ever wrote suggested that he had academic ability. He was a good study in the theatrical sense. He could mimic and use other people's ideas, but had none himself. He was just a talking parrot.

When a student in one of his classes had boldly remarked that the wording of his lectures seemed very similar to the text of a book by the theologian E. L. Mascall, Peters had brazenly turned the accusation on its head: 'It was vewy naughty of Ewic to use my lectures in his book without acknowledgement.'

By now he was calling himself Robert Parkin Peters and had contrived to be re-ordained under his new name – not, as he had told Trevor-Roper, in Washington State, by the Bishop of Olympia, but in Canada, by the Bishop of Toronto. This, so far as Peters was concerned, wiped the slate clean. But such was the complexity and the scope of the web he had woven that he remained vulnerable to anyone who might have known him in a previous life. On the staff at Trinity was a man who had been a resident in the same Toc H hostel during the war; whenever he came into the senior common room, Peters lowered his (usually booming) voice, and left as soon as he could find an excuse for doing so. Then, still in his first term, he was introduced to the formidable wife of Archdeacon Fotheringham, a Scottish Epis-copalian in the divinity faculty. She insisted that she had seen him somewhere in Scotland, notwithstanding his denial that he had ever set foot in that country, with its implication that nobody with any sense would do so. Her persistence prompted the Provost of Trinity to enquire into Peters's credentials. 'I have reason to suspect that Mr Peters is misrepresenting his qualifications,' the Provost wrote to the President of Magdalen, 'and I shall be glad of any information you can give me.' The Provost had also approached Lambeth Palace, to learn that the Archbishop of Canterbury had castigated Peters as 'this criminous clerk'.* This reply, together with the response from Magdalen, and from the university Registrar, who stated firmly that nobody of that name had taken a degree from Oxford since at least the eighteenth century, persuaded the Provost to dispense with Peters's services after only one term.

Peters fled Toronto at the end of the year, leaving behind a mass of debts. The student newspaper of the University of Toronto printed a limerick to mark his departure:

There once was a tutor at Trinity
Who no longer is teaching Divinity
For to talk about Gawd
Without M.A. Oxfawd
Is the most egregious assinity.

Peters's subsequent peregrinations across North America over the following five years were summarised in the reply sent to Cuthbert Simpson by his friend at Trinity College, the Reverend Eugene Fairweather:

After leaving us he served in Pittsburgh† ... and then appeared

---

* 'Criminous' can mean either criminal, as in a person guilty of a crime, or suspected of a crime.

† Peters is said to have introduced himself to the Bishop of Pittsburgh as the Bishop-elect of Trinidad.

more or less in succession in Hamilton, Vancouver and Victoria (first under the aegis of some 'Old Catholic' sect and then as a star student in the Provincial Normal School*), in Montreal (as a schoolmaster and featured preacher at the Church of the Advent, Westmount), in Detroit and Ann Arbor ... and at the College of Wooster ...

Having run up significant debts in Pittsburgh, Peters had made his way back across the border again, to Hamilton, Ontario, and fell in with the Old Catholics there, who appointed him their archimandrite, or chief representative – 'Exarch of the West' – in British Columbia. (An archimandrite is an honorific rank, only one level lower than a bishop, requiring celibacy.) Now styling himself 'Monsignor Peters', he was photographed in front of a large house for the *Vancouver News Herald*. The accompanying story announced that 'Mgr. Peters' had come to the Greater Vancouver area to establish an interdenominational college, to be known as 'The College of St Francis', described as 'a training school for young people who want to do Christian and social work at home or overseas'. The monsignor had launched an appeal to raise $10,000, requested that donations should be sent to him personally, and helpfully provided an address in Vancouver. A few days later the Roman Catholic archdiocese in Vancouver issued a statement dissociating itself from this venture. On 8 September 1950 the *Vancouver News Herald* printed a further story under the heading 'Warning Issued Against Fund Raiser'. Peters complained, but it was too late: 'The College of St Francis' was stillborn. Peters was then

---

* A teacher training college.

reported to be seeking work as a teacher in Cloverdale, British Columbia. While in the locality he kindly offered to validate some old documents for the university library in Vancouver, which were later found across the border in Seattle, on sale in an antiquarian bookshop.

Only days after the College of St Francis had expired, Peters reappeared over two thousand miles away, as Principal of the Consolidated School of Franklin, Quebec, where he would remain for sixteen months – for Peters, a comparatively long-lasting appointment. Maybe this small town (population approximately 1,000) was a good place to lie low. Then, according to Fairweather, he taught for a while in Montreal, before re-crossing the border to take up a teaching post in Detroit, followed by another in Ann Arbor. None of these lasted long. At some stage Peters visited New York, where he announced his acceptance of the bishopric of the Leeward Islands (a non-existent post, though there is a bishop of the Windward Islands) and obtained the necessary vestments on credit. Perhaps they were intended to impress – or merely to adorn his personage. He applied, unsuccessfully, for the post of General Secretary of the Australian branch of the Student Christian Movement. But he did succeed in obtaining a tutorial post at the College of Wooster, Ohio, thanks to his excellent qualifications, especially his degree in history (first-class honours) from Magdalen College, Oxford.

Peters was able to impress Americans and Canadians with his 'fund of Oxford gossip' – picked up, of course, while he was an undergraduate there. At Wooster he dazzled the local chapter of the American Association of University Women with a talk on life at Oxford University. Each of his lectures on Western civilisation had to be given twice, to accommodate

Robert Peters in the mid 1950s.

all those, both town and gown, who wanted to hear it. When he happened to mention in passing that he had taken a music degree from the University of Durham, he was invited to play the organ in the college chapel. He boasted of preaching off the cuff in St Paul's Cathedral, and preached several sermons at Wooster.* As Trevor-Roper had informed Hurstfield, Peters had abandoned his second wife on a train somewhere between Colombo, Ceylon, and Columbus, Ohio, and she had subsequently divorced him on grounds of desertion; by the time he reached Wooster he was presenting himself as an unmarried man. He asked a young American woman reading for a liberal arts degree if she would come out with him on a date. She agreed, but doubted the stories he told about his past. He seemed to her 'quite strange', with 'hypnotic eyes' and 'an oddly proportioned body'. She sought the advice of another Englishman on the staff, a lecturer in geography, who helped her to fend

---

* Afterwards a story about Peters at Wooster, 'The Polished Prof', was published in *Time* magazine.

off Peters's attentions. From Fairweather's account, it seems that this was a lucky escape:

> There were at least two women formally or semi-formally linked to him in England, another here and from Pittsburgh to Vancouver, another near-miss (only prevented by the fact that the priest who was asked to perform the ceremony knew about Peters) in Victoria, an informal arrangement (with the wife of a Dorval RCAF officer) in Detroit and (I think) another attempt, at least, in 1954–55, after his deportation from the USA and return to England ...

Trevor-Roper already knew from the Magdalen files that Peters had been deported from the United States after he had been unmasked at Wooster, and he was able to discover what had happened subsequently from the press cuttings. As Peters stepped off the liner *Italia* at Plymouth on 11 July 1953, he had been re-arrested by the English police. This time there would be no question of bail; the authorities were not going to risk losing him again. The *Daily Mirror* provided a vivid (perhaps imaginary) picture of the scene: 'Women wept as he embraced his aged father on the quayside.'* A young American student, described as 'a pretty eighteen year old', told the reporter, 'I just can't believe it.' Before being driven off to spend the weekend in a cell, Peters accepted a cigarette from the sergeant making the arrest. During the Atlantic crossing, readers were told, 'the handsome, well groomed Church of England curate' had been asked to take a service. According to the *Daily Mirror*, Peters

---

* From what little we know about Peters's relations with his father, this seems unlikely.

had already 'won the respect of all his fellow passengers on the first class deck', so that long before the service had begun the spacious lounge was packed with passengers. 'I've never enjoyed a service so much,' Mrs Lucy Stimson, from Philadelphia, was reported as saying. 'It was conducted in such a sympathetic way.'

The press tended to play up Peters's looks, just as they tended to exaggerate his scholarly ability. No doubt it helped sales to depict him as a handsome Romeo, almost irresistible to women. In fact, as the young woman at Wooster had attested, he was rather dumpy in appearance, shorter than average, plump and stiff-backed. It has to be conceded that a surprising number of women succumbed to his advances – but perhaps he operated on the often-quoted principle that if at first you don't succeed, you should try again, and keep trying until you do.

Peters was escorted by the police for trial to Inverness – the jurisdiction in which he had committed his alleged crime – where a crowd of locals and visitors was waiting on the platform to see him arrive. On 29 July he was sentenced to four months' imprisonment for bigamy. In mitigation, Peters admitted having married Hilda Brunton in 1943, but said that they had 'hardly lived together at all'. His solicitor argued that he had been unable to consummate his first marriage because he was impotent – perhaps not the ideal defence to a charge of bigamy. 'There can be no doubt,' the solicitor had told the court, 'that Mr Peters was not well mentally at the time.' Passing sentence, the sheriff had issued a stern reprimand: 'A man of your education and your calling, above all people, should have known the seriousness of the rites of marriage.' During the hearing it was stated that Peters 'still intended to go on studying for his Ph.D. degree'. This was the first (though not the last) mention of studying for a doctorate and seems in this instance to have been nothing more than a pious hope, intended to show that Peters was a man of scholarly character. It is most unlikely that he could have been admitted to a course of study for a higher degree without having first obtained an undergraduate degree.

Following his release late in 1953, Peters had taken a succession of jobs in schools as chaplain or history master. None lasted more than a few months. While teaching at Danes Hill Preparatory School, Oxshott, Surrey, he had wooed a local osteopath, Miss Ruth Cottle, taking her to a school dinner each week. They quickly become engaged; but she broke it off when she learned something of his history. It was 'a shock', she told a reporter from the *Daily Mirror*. 'To me he was a sound young man, a worthy member of the Church. I haven't seen him since. I don't want to.'

A former pupil at Danes Hill remembers Peters umpiring a cricket match, wearing a bib & dog collar under a cream linen jacket, a large floppy straw hat covering his thinning pate; there was some disagreement over his interpretation of the lbw law. He had an Austin 7 motorcar (the 'Baby Austin'), from which he extricated himself in a crab-like manner. While on the staff at Danes Hill Peters often officiated at morning prayers; after his sudden departure the headmaster was overheard telling parents that his leaving was matter of regret, if only because of his wonderful ability with spontaneous prayer.

In the summer of 1954 Peters suddenly appeared at the church of St Helen's, Burghwallis, a Yorkshire hamlet about seven miles north of Doncaster. The incumbent, Father John Willis Kidd, was dying of cancer; Peters, who had arrived as locum, took up residence in the Rectory, though it meant that Kidd had to make do with less space. The new man made an immediate impression, thanks to his silver tongue, commanding presence, and theatrical sermons. The ladies of the congregation swooned on him. It rapidly became known that he had strong connections with Oxford University, indeed was held in high regard there. Always fussy about his appearance, Peters ensured that his Doctor of Divinity tabs were on show. The general feeling in the parish was that they were lucky to have secured the services of such a man. Though Father Kidd was still alive, a campaign began to have Peters installed as his successor; and, encouraged by Peters, the congregation got up a petition to have him appointed as parish priest, but the Bishop of Sheffield was mysteriously slow to respond. Peters explained that such delay was typical of church bureaucracy. One of the churchwardens began to ask questions: why was such a brilliant preacher, so well-travelled, so learned and so very well qualified, so keen to be appointed to a remote rural parish? Could he not do better elsewhere? The indignant congregation turned on the churchwarden and demanded his resignation. Then Father Kidd died, and it became known that the Bishop was not minded to appoint Peters as Rector of Burgh-wallis. The injured candidate abruptly decamped: he drove away early one morning, leaving the congregation without a minister to take Sunday service.

At Burghwallis Peters had been joined by a young Australian woman, whom he introduced as his fiancée, to the disappointment of many. This was a widow, Mrs Janet Lascelles from New South Wales. Almost nothing is known of their courtship, but, as Trevor-Roper learned from Cuthbert Simpson, they were married at the Church of the Annunciation, just off Marble Arch in London, on 14 August 1954. Almost five years later, the vicar, the Reverend Gervase Bennett, would respond to a letter of enquiry from Trevor-Roper. Peters had given 'every sem-blance of piety', even asking for a special nuptial mass – a detail that delighted Trevor-Roper.* 'He called himself a schoolmaster and I had no idea that he had ever been in Holy Orders,' wrote Bennett. 'I would not of course have performed the ceremony had I known that he had previously been married.' (In those days it was unusual for divorced persons to be allowed to marry in church.) This new union was of bewilderingly short duration: after only sixteen days the third Mrs Peters returned to her parents in Sydney, having been dismissed by her new husband. A year later she spoke to the same *Daily Mirror* reporter. She had not heard from Peters since she left England and, like Ruth Cottle, she seemed shocked by her experience of him. 'It leaves a horrible taste in the mouth,' she said. 'I still can't reconcile it with the man I knew.'

Peters had not given up on marriage, however. He took a job at a school in Street, Somerset, where he met a shorthand teacher, Margaret Britton; after only eleven days' acquaintance he had offered her his hand and been accepted. Then he disap-peared, leaving no forwarding address. Miss Britton was obliged to return the engagement ring that he had given her, after learn-ing that the cheque with which it had been purchased had not been honoured.

At a school in Reigate, Surrey, Peters courted the art teacher, Pamela Haigh. She accepted his proposal of marriage; but, like Miss Cottle, broke off the engagement when she became aware

---

* Bennett was irritated when he learned, sometime after, that Peters had applied to Westminster Cathedral for reception into the Roman Catholic Church.

of his unsavoury past. In the eighteen months since his release from prison he had wooed and won no fewer than four women, one of whom he had actually married. He was already betrothed to yet another young woman when he was arrested again.

Peters's second trial took place at the London Sessions, towards the end of August 1955. In the dock he appeared smartly dressed, in grey suit and – a prescient detail – Magdalen College tie. He was charged with wilfully causing a false statement to be inserted in a marriage register, having described himself as 'a bachelor' in his application for a licence to marry Mrs Janet Lascelles. In fact he was by then divorced, since his first wife had divorced him for desertion in 1949, and his second wife had also divorced him – though their marriage, being bigamous, was anyway invalid. After consulting three dictionaries, the chairman of the London Quarter Sessions, Mr A. W. Cockburn, QC, decided that a bachelor was an unmarried man, and that a divorced man could therefore be described as a bachelor. The prosecution case was 'a muddle', Cockburn ruled. 'The defendant may have told a lie to the clergyman, but the allegation here is that he made a false statement for the purpose of entry in a marriage register.' He directed the jury to find Peters not guilty of perjury.

But Peters was not so lucky the next day, when he was convicted of obtaining an engagement ring priced at £36 by passing a false cheque and jailed for six months; he was then jailed for a further six months for stealing a motorcar. Peters had bought the car from a garage in Woodford on a hire-purchase agreement, but failed to pay the first two instalments. The car was traced to Street, in Somerset, where Peters was found to have traded it in part exchange for another. The court heard that Peters had been ordained a Church of England priest in 1942. He was said to be the author of a book entitled *Know Yourself*.*

The *Daily Mirror* devoted four columns to the story, under the headline 'ROMEO OF THE CHURCH SWEPT 7 WOMEN OFF THEIR FEET'. For the popular press, the cocktail of religion and illicit sex was always alluring. Peters could be depicted as a stock character, the naughty vicar. His story was in some ways reminiscent of that of Harold Davidson, Rector of Stiffkey, whose zeal for the rescue of 'fallen' young women had led to a prosecution for immorality by a Church court in 1932. One decisive piece of evidence against Davidson had been a striking photograph of him in clerical dress reaching out towards a fifteen-year-old girl, her back to the camera; she clutched a shawl to her bosom, but was otherwise nude, her bottom bare to the camera. In his defence, Davidson claimed to have assumed that she was wearing a bathing suit. The court had rejected his pleas and found him guilty. Defrocked and bankrupt, Davidson was reduced to making a public exhibition of himself. For a while he appeared on the Blackpool seafront, notionally being roasted in a glass-fronted oven while a mechanised devil prodded him with a pitchfork. When interest in this performance waned, he began appearing in Skegness with caged lions, in a show billed as 'Daniel in a modern lion's den'; unfortunately, he stepped on a lion's tail and was fatally mauled. In his account of the inter-war years, A. J. P. Taylor wrote that the rector's case 'offered a parable of the age', and argued that Davidson had attracted more attention than the Archbishop of Canterbury. 'Which man deserves a greater place in the history books?'

---

*I have been unable to trace this book, and suspect that it never existed.

The *Daily Mirror* report of Peters's trial described how his current fiancée, Margaret Coleman, a 'fair-haired, bespectacled Girl Guide leader', had attended the trial in the public gallery, wearing a flowered dress and the diamond engagement ring that he had given her. 'When Peters was sentenced, he glanced up at Margaret. She bent down, cupped her hands, and covered her face.'

Following Peters's earlier conviction, the Archbishop of Canterbury himself had circulated a memorandum about Peters, declaring him 'incapable of holding clerical preferment'. His second conviction appears to have been the last straw and Peters was 'formally and publicly deprived of his orders': in other words, he was 'defrocked'. In the Anglican Church, this process is extremely rare; Peters is said to have been the last Anglican clergyman to be thus formally unfrocked. The ceremony took place in Wells Cathedral and was conducted by the Bishop of Bath and Wells – no doubt because Peters had been living in Bath for a while.

But even as one bishop taketh away, another giveth. While serving his sentence Peters had been visited in prison by the Bishop of Birmingham, the Right Reverend Leonard Wilson, who had taken an interest in him, to the extent that he employed him as a secretary on his release early in 1956. It was not long before Peters noticed that Wilson was in the habit of signing his letters unread. One day he had brought the bishop a pile of letters for his signature, in the midst of which was an excellent testimonial that Peters had written for himself.

As Trevor-Roper knew from Joel Hurstfield, Peters had appeared at University College, London, at the beginning of the autumn term 1957, claiming to be an MA Oxon, and had registered as a postgraduate student there. Simultaneously (as Hurstfield discovered) Peters had registered as an undergraduate at Birkbeck College 'and therefore achieved the rare distinction of being an undergraduate and a postgraduate at the same time'. Then Peters had made his way to Oxford, arriving halfway through the 1957 Michaelmas term in order to begin reading for his B.Litt. There he had met the Regius Professor, to complain of persecution by the Bishop of Oxford. There, too, he had married the fourth Mrs Peters, Marie Baillie from New Zealand, also twenty-two years old, as her predecessor the second Mrs Peters had been, though Peters was by this time forty. Technically this marriage, like his second, was bigamous, as Peters's divorce from the third Mrs Peters had not then been concluded.

Intermittent news of Peters's progress reached Oxford in the weeks following his flight from the city in February 1959. The *Daily Express* reported that Peters had indeed gone to Derbyshire, as he had told his supervisor Miss Major, to stay in a country house with some family friends of his wife; but that he had been asked to go elsewhere when his host, a local magistrate, had been made aware of his disgraceful past. According to the *Express* report, Peters's wife had been torn between staying and leaving; but was eventually persuaded to leave by Peters, who told her that her place was by his side, at least until his tangled affairs were cleared up. She had left, weeping, in Peters's old black car. A fortnight later Hurstfield wrote to tell Trevor-Roper that Peters had taken shelter at St Deiniol's Library, Hawarden, on the Welsh border, which he described as 'a kind of study centre for Anglican clergymen and others'.* In this letter Hurstfield

---

* Another member of Magdalen, the young Alan Bennett, was working there around the time.

speculated that Peters might be moving out of the Faculty of Arts into the Faculty of Theology, 'because there must be vast opportunities if he is not yet too well known'.

Acting on this intelligence, Trevor-Roper wrote to Sir Charles Gladstone, squire of Hawarden, whose son William had been a pupil of his at 'the House'; indeed, Sir Charles himself had been a Christ Church man before the First World War. Trevor-Roper warned the baronet about the cuckoo in his nest. Sir Charles contacted the local police, but they, like their colleagues in Oxford, were too slow: by the time they arrived, the bird had flown. That weekend a story appeared in the tabloid *Sunday Pictorial*: 'PETERS THE PARSON CLEARS OUT'. Once again he was emigrating. 'My wild days are over,' he was quoted as saying. 'From now on I am going to lead a quiet respectable life abroad ... I have been a fool. Yet my only wish has been to serve God and be recognised academically ... I have left behind three former wives – but take with me the <u>only</u> woman I have ever loved.'

The following Sunday a double-page spread appeared in the same newspaper, seemingly written by Peters himself: 'MY YEARS WITH FOUR WOMEN'. Below the banner headline was an emboldened editorial:

> BEFORE HE FLED Britain for a new life abroad last week, forty-one year old Robert Parkin Peters – Peters the Parson – told the shameful story of his life to the Sunday Pictorial.
> FOR THE FIRST TIME he revealed the secret behind his four marriages and his deposement from office as an Anglican priest by the Archbishop of Canterbury.
> FOR THE FIRST TIME he told the story of his last twelve hectic, law-dodging years.

IT IS THE STORY of an extraordinary man – a man of God who left the path of truth and honesty. And it is now told for the first time – by Peters the Parson himself.

Peters's confessional observed all the conventions of the genre. He provided prurient details, admitted mistakes, expressed remorse (possibly the only time he did so), described hardship and invited sympathy. His piteous apologia was enough to bring a tear to even the most cynical eye. Some of it might even have been true.

He had, he said, been born 'a hopeless cripple' and spent the first nine years of his life in a steel frame. 'My father did not like me – he made me feel inferior,' he wrote. 'When that wretched frame came off, and I took my first few faltering steps, I was determined to show the world I was brilliant – and make my father proud of me.' He had worked 'desperately' to make up for the lost years when he had been unable to study. It had been 'a high point of my life' when he had been ordained deacon in 1941. His first wife, Hilda Brunton, had been his parents' choice. 'I did not love Hilda, but I was young and inexperienced.' It had been only after they were married that he discovered he was 'psychologically incapable of making love'. The same had been true of his next two marriages. 'Only my last union has been successful. And they call me "the Romeo in a dog collar".'

In his account of his career, Peters did not pretend that he had always been entirely candid: 'I lied, I tricked, but I remained faithful to God.' He had fled the country rather than face trial for bigamy 'because I saw myself helpless again, trapped in a spinal frame'. When he was sacked by Wooster, 'a thousand students demonstrated at the college, shouting, "Peters must stay", but it was no use.' He gave a pitiful picture of life on the run, moving from job to job. 'Sometimes I lasted weeks, sometimes days. Sooner or later, people found out about me.' His most startling revelation was that after he had been defrocked, the Archbishop of Canterbury himself had granted him a private interview: 'I found him sympathetic, but firm. He told me that I could always earn a living some other way.' (This was, of course, a complete fiction.)

Peters admitted 'the terrible mess I have made of my life'. The piece ended in a touching peroration:

> When I was sacked from Oxford I knew the sands had run out for me.
>
> But I had found the first REAL thing in my life. It was my marriage to Marie, a success in every way …
>
> We made the decision to start again overseas, without lies, without fraud.
>
> For twelve years I have been the elusive 'Peters the Parson', yet all I ever wanted was to work hard and lead a settled life.
>
> I cannot stay away from the church, nor can I stay away from learning.
>
> Yes, there is still a lot to do in life. But now I will go about it honestly, with Marie by my side.
>
> PETERS THE PARSON IS DEAD – AND MY CRAZY YEARS OF FOLLY ARE OVER.

FIVE

In which the parson finds a saviour

Six months passed before any further report of Peters reached Trevor-Roper. Then, in the middle of September 1959, he received a note from Cuthbert Simpson, by this time Dean of Christ Church. 'You will be interested to hear that our friend Peters has turned up in Dublin as "Dr Peters",' wrote Simpson. Apparently Peters had called on one of the Anglican churches there, informed the vicar that he was an Anglican priest and asked to be allowed to celebrate holy communion. The vicar had been canny enough to refer the matter to the Archbishop of Dublin, George Simms. A few days later Simms had telephoned the vicar. 'Do you want to know what the Archbishop of Canterbury has to say about your friend Peters?' he asked.

Simms instructed the startled vicar to tell Peters that he, the archbishop, had 'heard of him', assuming that this hint would be enough to send him packing – but Peters took this as a welcome, or at least affected to do so. 'I am very surprised, but interested that the archbishop should have heard of me,' he replied. 'When the situation has clarified itself, and if I am able to secure some more or less permanent teaching, I shall be very glad to avail myself of His Grace's kind offer to see me.'

Having submitted his services to the Anglican Archbishop of Dublin, describing himself as an Anglican, Peters submitted his services to the Roman Catholic Archbishop of Dublin, describing himself as a Catholic. This was no more successful, perhaps because the two archbishops, being on courteous terms,* had compared notes.

It was time to move on. Peters next reappeared in Canada, as Trevor-Roper would learn in another note from Simpson, relaying news from his Toronto informant, the Reverend Eugene Fairweather, whose boss, the Provost of Trinity College, had been attending a heads of college meeting in Montreal, and had found himself seated next to Wilfred Lockhart, Principal of United College, Winnipeg. United College was still reeling from a mass resignation, following the dismissal of a left-leaning professor, Harry S. Crowe – an incident which, so protesters argued, had violated the security of academic tenure. Lockhart proudly informed the Provost that he had managed to secure the services of 'a distinguished Oxford historian', an important addition to their depleted history department. When the Provost casually asked his name, Lockhart replied, 'Robert P. Peters' – prompting the Provost to swallow hard and tell him all. Several days later the Provost had received an almost fulsomely grateful letter from Lockhart, with effusive thanks for saving him from 'a catastrophic blunder'.

Soon afterwards a member of the Faculty of Arts at Trinity College responsible for assessing manuscripts submitted for publication grants received one entitled *Oculus Episcopi: A Study*

---

* Trevor-Roper believed that the two archbishops were cousins, the type of detail in which he delighted. Sadly, he seems to have been wrong in this case.

of an English Archdeaconry in the Early Seventeenth Century by Robert P. Peters, of the (Roman Catholic) University of Ottawa. Recognising the name, he immediately contacted the Provost, who telephoned the University of Ottawa and asked to speak to the Rector. The latter allowed that he had had on his staff since September a fine English scholar named Peters, who held, among other degrees, a Ph.D. from the University of Washington. The Provost again told the whole Peters story. The shocked Rector dismissed Peters without delay.

A letter arrived in Trevor-Roper's in tray from Peters's former B.Litt. supervisor, Kathleen Major. A Canadian professor from another college in Toronto had written to her about an Englishman who had applied to read for a Ph.D.; he had been, so the professor wrote, 'a bit vague about his early qualifications', claiming that 'financial reasons' had prevented him from completing his B.Litt. degree in Oxford. By now it seemed almost inevitable that the prospective student would be Robert Peters. Later Trevor-Roper learned that Peters had also applied to read for a Ph.D. at McGill University, Montreal, and had been accepted; but he had been recognised by two of the historians there and quickly got rid of. 'He seems to have been a sort of academic Trelawney, with the same fascination for the opposite sex,'* one of them wrote to Trevor-Roper.

---

* Edward John Trelawny, author of *Adventures of a Younger Son* (1831), boasted to his friends Byron and Shelley that he had deserted from the navy as a young man, formed a band of pirates and married an Arab girl, later poisoned by a jealous rival. His stories about himself usually contained an element of truth, though much embellished. Biographers have been divided about whether or not he came to believe the fictions that he created.

By this time there can have been few universities in Canada where Peters had not appeared at some time or other. When the University of Guelph was set up in Ontario a few years later, Peters would be one of the very first to apply for a post there.

Towards the end of the month more news of Peters arrived from Fairweather: 'Your friend Mr Peters is in jail in Montreal at the moment, fighting deportation on the ground of moral turpitude, or some such thing.' (In fact the deportation order was granted on grounds that he was 'an undesirable person' within the meaning of the Immigration Act.) Meanwhile the Peters family had been blessed with a son, a possible reason for the authorities to show clemency; and perhaps they did, because in a further bulletin a month later Simpson reported that Peters had been extricated from jail and was now in the hands of psychologists, who had pronounced that, if he were to rebuild his life, it was essential that he should be allowed to take a degree of some kind. The Canadian authorities seemed unconvinced by this enlightened advice.

Early in May, Peters and his wife were sighted disembarking from a transatlantic liner in Ireland – 'just ahead of a deportation order from Canada', reported the *Daily Express*, in a story entitled 'PARSON PETERS AND MARIE STEP OFF BOAT'. In a photograph accompanying the article, the husband kept his eyes down from the camera, while the wife looked startled. Pressed for a statement, Peters replied, 'I have absolutely nothing to say.' Some while afterwards, Cuthbert Simpson learned that he had consulted an eminent barrister about the possibility of a libel suit against the *Daily Express*, though he did not take this any further – which was probably just as well, because there was nothing in the article that could not be verified.

On the move again: Peters in search of new worlds to conquer.

Now that he was back in the Old World, Peters was not slow in applying for work. He seemed to be on his way to Leeds as a research student, until the head of department there, Professor John Le Patourel, visiting Oxford for a Jesus College gaudy, heard enough about him to reconsider. Trevor-Roper only learned this many years later, in a letter from a friend, the historian Richard Cobb – an eccentric even by donnish standards, a prodigious drinker and an uninhibited gossip – who had taught at Leeds before he came to Oxford.

Seek, and ye shall find. After so many disappointments, Peters now found a saviour in Gordon Rupp, Professor of Ecclesiastical History and head of the Department of Theology at Manchester

University. Rupp was a Methodist preacher, a small man with simple tastes, who enjoyed fish and chips with ginger beer. As a boy he had stood on a box to preach the gospel in Finsbury Park, and even late in life he travelled all over the country to speak in remote rural chapels. Rupp was a very different type of man from Trevor-Roper: kind, perhaps a little unworldly. 'I am bound to say that had I known the full story in the beginning, we might not have taken him,' he would admit later; but at this stage he knew only that Peters had been in trouble at Oxford about his qualifications for his B.Litt. degree. He felt that Peters should be given 'a fresh start'. Manchester was one of the few universities where it was possible to take an MA without first having taken a BA. Here at last was an opportunity for Peters to gain a genuine qualification, to supplement those imaginary ones that had for so many years embellished his curriculum vitae. In October 1960 he was admitted to read for an MA by thesis at Manchester, while his wife began teaching at a local school, working to support the family. After so many years on the run, Peters had at last found a refuge, perhaps even sanctuary.

Trevor-Roper would come to believe that, in accepting Peters for an MA, Rupp had been influenced by the report of the Canadian psychologists. A letter from a British psychiatrist, dated only a month after Peters and his wife arrived from Canada, may be relevant, too; it was in Peters's possession, and perhaps he solicited it as an unusual form of testimonial. (The letter came to light years later, when Peters sent a copy to the President of Magdalen, in a bid to be rehabilitated there.) The writer was James Arthur Hadfield (born 1882), former Consultant in Psychological Medicine and Lecturer in Psychopathology and Mental Hygiene in the University of London. Evidently Peters had seen, or been sent to see, Hadfield at some point in the past. 'I was treating this patient some years ago for fear of his father,' wrote Hadfield. 'The treatment was so far quite successful in so far as he got rid of all his fears.' The letter, written in an elderly hand, is in places difficult to decipher, but the gist is clear:

> The abolition of fear however released the repressed aggressiveness and resentment against his father. In the normal course we would then have directed this aggressiveness towards the development of his will power and self-confidence.
>
> Unfortunately [at this point came the first?] prosecution, and treatment had to stop mid-way. Naturally the aggressiveness and [defiance?], left unsublimated at this stage, took abnormal forms and continued to do so for some years.
>
> But I am convinced that his case was a treatable condition, and I am confident that if treatment had not been broken off, he would have been cured.
>
> I see no reason therefore why he should not still be curable, if in fact he does have further treatments; for his case, in my opinion, is not of a constitutional type, but is due to his unfortunate and undesirable upbringing.

It is difficult to assess the value of this professional opinion. On the one hand, Dr Hadfield had been a respected figure in child and adolescent psychiatry in the early years of the Tavistock Clinic; on the other, he was in his late seventies by the time he wrote this letter and perhaps had lost some of his sharpness. Moreover, his approach to his work no longer found the acceptance that it once commanded; after his death in 1967, he would be criticised for his 'reductive attempts to recover childhood trauma'. It is worth remarking, too, that Hadfield, like most psychiatrists, was obliged to rely on what his patient had told him; and Peters had practised to deceive.

Peters judged that the time was ripe for him to resume his career as an Anglican clergyman, donning a dog collar and officiating at church services near his home in Altrincham and elsewhere, while he continued working for a higher degree. He ingratiated himself with the Bishop of Manchester, William Greer, and began serving as his chaplain. Years later, the then university Librarian, Dr F. W. Ratcliffe, would provide Trevor-Roper with an account of a visit from Peters, who had called at the library bearing an introduction from Professor Rupp. Ratcliffe had risen to his feet to greet him. Like so many others, he was completely taken in by this beaming, affable cleric, whose talk was larded with academic and scriptural references. Peters asked grandly what he might do for the library: he said that he was considering setting up a special fund to purchase a collection of books in his name. To Ratcliffe, he seemed almost a caricature of a learned clergyman, to the extent that it did not seem incongruous when he conferred a blessing on the Librarian before making his departure.

No more news of Robert Peters reached Oxford for the next couple of years. Perhaps he was knuckling down to work in Manchester. He was certainly adept at recycling. In April 1962 an article appeared under Peters's name in the *Journal of Ecclesiastical History*, 'The Administration of the Archdeaconry of St Albans, 1580–1625' – the same, safely dull subject that Peters had chosen for his Oxford B.Litt. While in Canada Peters had tried to publish a manuscript on this topic; a year later in England a short monograph (not more than eighty pages, excluding the appendix and the bibliography) was published by Manchester

University Press, entitled *Oculus Episcopi: Administration in the Archdeaconry of St Albans, 1580–1625*. This was adjudged 'a competent book' in the *Journal of Theological Studies* by the Cambridge historian Geoffrey Elton – faint praise perhaps, but then Elton was not normally considered an indulgent reviewer. After conferring with Kathleen Major, Trevor-Roper came to believe that most, if not all of it had been written by Mrs Peters; though she would later deny this, and of course it was difficult to prove. 'It does not display as much of the obvious inaccuracy that was in the draft thesis as I saw it before the debacle,' Miss Major would write to Trevor-Roper, after reading the published work. She shared Trevor-Roper's view that Peters was not a suitable candidate for a higher degree: 'I think Professor Rupp let his desire to rehabilitate a psychiatric case run away with him.'

Someone who chose not to identify himself (or herself) sent Rupp a dossier of damaging newspaper cuttings about Peters, which he took to the Vice-Chancellor. Though shocked by what the cuttings revealed, the two men agreed that, having come so far with the intention of giving Peters the chance of rehabilitation, they should press on. Rupp warned Peters sternly that he must not continue to impersonate a clergyman. But if his supervisor had not lost faith in him, his wife had, after five years of marriage, and she returned with their small son to her native New Zealand, to commence a career as a legitimate academic. She would play no further part in this story.* In a letter conveying the sad news to Rupp, Peters seemed most peeved that she had taken the dog with her.

---

*In 2018 her son and his wife advertised on the internet for information about 'Professor Robert Peters'.

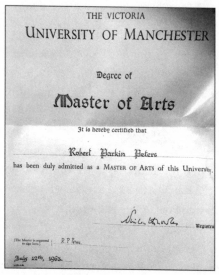

THE VICTORIA
UNIVERSITY OF MANCHESTER

Degree of

Master of Arts

It is hereby certified that

Robert Parkin Peters

has been duly admitted as a MASTER OF ARTS of this University.

Registra

[The Master is requested to sign here.] R. P. Peters.

July 12th, 1963.

Peters's only legitimate qualification, an MA certificate awarded in July 1963. Trevor-Roper believed that he had been granted this degree out of a misplaced sense of kindness, possibly in response to threats of suicide.

In July 1963 Peters was granted an MA, his first and, as it would turn out, his only qualification from a British university. With these precious letters after his name, and Rupp's encouragement, he began to attend academic conferences, take part in seminars and write more articles for learned journals on obscure subjects. He was emboldened enough to appear in Oxford, at a meeting of the Ecclesiastical History Society, and even to make a contribution to the discussion, although, according to the report that reached Trevor-Roper via Kathleen Major, he did not impress his auditors. Meanwhile he began searching for paid work, to provide an income, now that he could no longer rely on his wife's salary as a teacher. Among the many posts he applied for were jobs with the Norfolk and Norwich Record Office, the Cambridgeshire Record Office and the Cumbrian branch of the Workers' Educational Association – unsuccessfully in every case. He seems to have applied, too, for a number of jobs in schools, for in June 1964 Trevor-Roper received a letter from Logie Bruce Lockhart, headmaster of Gresham's. In response to a request for a reference, Bruce Lockhart had warned that Peters should never be employed in a school where he would come into contact with girls. Though this advice had been confidential, Peters had somehow discovered it, and was now threatening to sue Bruce Lockhart for defamation. In case of legal action, Bruce Lockhart asked Trevor-Roper for evidence of Peters's misdemeanours, with names and dates if possible.

'The fantasies, forgeries and impostures of "The Reverend" Robert Parkin Peters would fill a book,' replied Trevor-Roper. 'As I am just beginning to examine for the Final Schools, you will not expect me, I hope, to write a book.' But he did provide a synopsis of what he knew – 'a most helpful and illuminating document,' according to the headmaster. 'It confirms much of what I believed and I can only think that if Peters brings an action for slander I must, indeed, be ingenious to have gone beyond the truth.' He then commented, 'I should very much like to have met the man, who must have some remarkable qualities.'

Peters was in search of a replacement for his departed wife, as Trevor-Roper would learn from a further letter from Bruce Lockhart. A local Norfolk cleric had telephoned the headmaster out of concern for his young daughter, who had accepted Peters's proposal of marriage. She and her mother had met Peters while on holiday in Eastbourne, where he was teaching English to foreign students. (He was sacked after four weeks, but refused to leave until he had served the eight weeks allowed for in his contract.) Peters had repeatedly sent the vicar's wife flowers, as well as showing her around local churches. On being told that the girl was having difficulty getting into university, he had offered his help, boasted of his contacts in the academic world and promised that he could obtain a place for her. He had accompanied the mother and daughter back to Norfolk, where the then unsuspecting vicar had invited him to officiate in his own church. Peters had promptly offered his hand to the girl, who had accepted. The mother seemed delighted at this development, though Peters, then forty-six, seemed a little old for their daughter, who was still a teenager. The father was much less keen, and his anxious enquiries about his prospective son-in-law had led him to contact Bruce Lockhart, who quickly convinced him that his fears were justified. Afterwards, when the vicar had relayed what he had heard about Peters to his daughter, she had been so upset that she had become ill, and refused to believe it until she was brought to see Bruce Lockhart and heard the truth for herself. She had then broken off the engagement. Once again, Peters had been thwarted at the last moment. He had already gone so far as to apply to teach at a girls' school nearby in Cromer, and had put in a separate job application on behalf of his future bride.

Despite this reverse, Peters's enthusiasm for matrimony remained undiminished. Around this time he is said to have married an academic from King's College, London, though the marriage was soon discovered to be bigamous. Nothing more is known of this intriguing episode. The report stems from the dossier kept by Gavin White, the Canadian who had known Peters in Toronto, by now himself an ordained minister.

Rupp agreed to act as supervisor to Peters for a higher degree, a Ph.D. His subject, apparently suggested by Rupp, was 'King James VI and I as a Theologian'. One can only speculate about Peters's motive for wanting a higher degree; perhaps he hoped that a Ph.D. would cover up his lack of more basic qualifications. In those days most aspirant historians would begin a period of specialised study after taking an undergraduate degree, but by no means all would go on to write a thesis and take a doctorate. College fellowships were awarded at such a young age that there was no time to do so beforehand, and no necessity after. Indeed, a doctorate was regarded as a mark of failure, since in general only those who had failed to obtain a fellowship possessed them; and in England (though not in America) it was regarded as somewhat *infra dig* to use the title 'Dr'. Few in the older generation possessed a doctorate: Trevor-Roper did not, nor did A. J. P. Taylor, the best-known historian in Britain at the time. The Cambridge historian F. H. Hinsley (later Sir Harry Hinsley) did not even possess a first degree, since in 1939 he had been recruited into Bletchley Park as a cryptanalyst while still an undergraduate and elected a college Fellow after the war. His lack of a degree did not prevent him, in due course, becoming Master of his college and then Vice-Chancellor of the university. It was only later, in the more bureaucratic 1970s, that a doctorate would become a requirement for academic appointments.

Hinsley had been born in the same year as Peters, whose contribution to the war effort had been limited to a few months' part-time fire-watching. Work on his Ph.D. would occupy Peters for a number of years; meanwhile he continued to search for paid employment. In October 1964, after a succession of failed applications, he secured a position within the prestigious Cambridge

Group for the History of Population and Social Structure, run by Peter Laslett of Trinity and E. A. Wrigley of Peterhouse (later Sir Tony Wrigley, President of the British Academy). He came with a very impressive list of testimonials, 'none of which', as Laslett later confessed to Trevor-Roper, 'we investigated'. Through Wrigley, who was at that time Bursar of Peterhouse, Peters obtained accommodation belonging to the college in Fitzwilliam Street. But this success proved temporary: he was discharged after less than three months, after showing himself to be 'entirely unsuited' to the kind of work (statistics and analysis of social structures) that was the essence of the Group's activities. Trevor-Roper heard this story from the Librarian at Lambeth Palace and wrote to Laslett for more details. Laslett admitted that he and Wrigley had been 'gravely embarrassed' when the story of Peters's previous career was 'forced upon us', very soon after he had begun work there; presumably someone had sent him a selection of newspaper clippings, perhaps indeed the same someone who had sent a selection to Rupp. Laslett wrote to Manchester to enquire why no reference to these worrying facts about Peters's past had been made in the testimonial; and was told that, on the contrary, reference to them *had* been made in the testimonial. Peters, to whom the testimonial had been given, had obviously opened it, read it and, finding it unsatisfactory, made use of Rupp's typewriter and headed paper to write his own version, more appropriate to his needs.

Once again finding himself unemployed, Peters began a new round of applications, supported by genuine testimonials from Rupp. 'We feel that, as a Christian faculty, it is our business to try and help him to make good with his very real gifts,' Rupp wrote in one of these. Peters applied to become an assistant archivist at the Ipswich and East Suffolk Record Office; a local editor for Shropshire for the Victoria County History; an assistant examiner for the Oxford and Cambridge Examination Board; a Stanley A. Cook Bye-Fellow at Gonville and Caius College, Cambridge; a lecturer in history at University College, Dublin; a lecturer in religious studies at the University of Ibadan, Nigeria; a senior research fellow at the Warburg Institute* in London; a resident tutor in Norfolk for the University of Cambridge Board of Extra-Mural Studies; an assistant professor at Notre Dame University of Nelson, British Columbia; and no doubt numerous other posts. In a personal letter to the professor of history at the Memorial University, St John's, Newfoundland, Rupp admitted that Peters had

> an unfortunate record of past follies, which I am afraid is bound to catch up with him, but he has made a clean breast of it to us and here in Manchester we have done all we could to encourage him to make a new start. We are anxious that he should do so and are all the more anxious because he has many fine gifts.

If necessary, Rupp was willing to write giving the fullest details of 'these unfortunate happenings' in Peters's earlier career, 'but may I say again that we here believe these follies are behind him and he deserves a good chance'. In writing that Peters had 'made

---

* 'I should certainly approach his case with very great caution,' advised Boase, who was on the Warburg's management committee. After interviewing Peters, the director, Professor E. H. Gombrich, commented, 'I definitely had the impression that he is psychologically not quite in order.' Peters claimed that he had been runner-up for the post.

a clean breast of it', Rupp was being disingenuous: in fact he had known nothing of Peters's history of wrongdoings until confronted with the evidence of the newspaper cuttings.

Even Rupp, however, drew the line when asked whether Peters was a suitable person to exercise pastoral care for young people:

> I am afraid that I do not think he is, in any way, qualified to be the Warden of a university hostel that requires elements of dependability and wisdom which I think is [*sic*] utterly lacking in this case.

Rupp received a complaint from Mowbrays bookshop in Cambridge: they had not been paid for books which Peters had obtained from them on credit. 'If I were you I should put this right as soon as possible,' Rupp advised Peters. The Chief Education Officer for Cambridgeshire, having received a testimonial from Rupp supporting Peters's application for a temporary teaching post, queried his statement that Peters had done a certain amount of supply teaching during the time he was in Manchester, 'with considerable acceptance and good practical results', since he understood from the Chief Education Officer for Manchester that Peters had been employed there for only a few days. He informed Rupp, in strictest confidence, that Peters's name was on the list published by the Department of Education and Science of persons determined by the Secretary of State to be unsuitable for employment as teachers. He thought Rupp should know that his reference was being used by Peters 'to commend him for an activity which he is legally unable to follow'.

'His library always impressed.' Unfortunately the
books had not always been paid for.

Peters kept his flat in Fitzwilliam Street as a base. Since
moving to Cambridge he had begun officiating at church services in the area, to the extent that the Bishop of Ely found it
necessary to issue a warning to all clergy in his diocese that Peters
was no longer qualified to act as a clergyman in holy orders in

the Church of England. Peters sought an interview with the bishop, who declined to see him. As he had done in the past, Peters argued that his exclusion from the Church was a matter of doctrine, whereas in reality it was one of conduct. But his words fell on stony ground: he was obliged to give the bishop 'my assurance that I shall not seek to officiate in an Anglican church, nor represent myself as an Anglican clergyman'.

Peters's promise was perhaps carefully phrased not to be a direct lie, because once again he was flirting with Rome. He was said to have received financial support from a devout Catholic lady in Manchester, to whom he had represented himself as having 'forfeited all' by his spiritual conversion to Catholicism. The headmaster of Gresham's reported on a visit from the mother superior of a nearby convent, with whom Peters had spent some considerable time locked in theological argument. He had told her that he was toying with the idea of becoming an Old Catholic and seemed to think that (though married) he might become a priest in that church. The mother superior became suspicious of him. She told the headmaster of her belief that Peters might be impotent, a theory new to him and 'mildly surprising from such a source'. The mother superior may have been unaware that Peters had fathered a son; it seems possible that he hinted at sexual problems as an excuse to explain his otherwise inexplicable behaviour.

In 1965, at an international historical congress in Vienna, Trevor-Roper, dozing through a series of grave statements about heresy in the seventeenth century, was startled into wakefulness when the French president of the session called upon 'Monsieur le Professeur Peters de l'Université de Manchester' to speak, and looked up, to see his 'old friend' on his feet, ready to commence a learned intervention. When Peters discerned Trevor-Roper, he turned green and modestly disclaimed the title of professor before speaking, then quickly departed at the end. At the reception given afterwards by the British ambassador, Peters began to proposition Trevor-Roper's stepdaughter Xenia, then aged twenty-one (by this time he was forty-seven), until he discovered who she was. The next day he was found to have left the congress prematurely.

Trevor-Roper would later describe Peters's contribution to the congress as 'utterly worthless: meaningless, niggling, unverifiable pedantry whose sole purpose was to advertise the speaker'. It reminded him, he said, of Jim Dixon's article in *Lucky Jim*, entitled 'The Economic Influence of the Developments in Shipbuilding Techniques, 1450 to 1485', which Dixon himself confessed was 'perfect ... in that it crystallised the article's niggling mindlessness, its funereal parade of yawn-enforcing facts, the pseudo-light it threw upon non-problems'.

After the congress Trevor-Roper wrote to the Registrar of Manchester University, to ask how Peters had come to be there, since participation at such events was supposed to be confined to bona fide historians: 'I write because Peters is an applicant for every academic post in history which is advertised in the English-speaking world and I am continually being consulted about him.' In reply, the Registrar confessed to having had 'very considerable reservations' about Peters when he had applied for acceptance at Manchester, and told Trevor-Roper that he had expressed his concern to the professors who were proposing to accept him. He forwarded Trevor-Roper's letter to the congress organiser, the medievalist E. F. Jacob, whose relations with Trevor-Roper had become strained while he was in Oxford as Chichele Professor of History from 1950 to 1961. 'I am not clear what particular *locus standi* Professor Trevor-Roper has in this matter,' replied Jacob, obviously annoyed by his intervention. As well as to Jacob, the Registrar had also forwarded Trevor-Roper's letter to Rupp, leading to an exchange of letters between Peters's persecutor and his defender. The exchange was polite, though Rupp thought Trevor-Roper uncharitable and Trevor-Roper thought Rupp 'a great ninny'.

'It is, of course, a very vexed question as to whether anybody with such a past can be given a chance of this kind with the risk of damaging one's university reputation and the business of giving scandal in the academic world,' Rupp wrote to Trevor-Roper, 'but I think you will agree that, if there is to be any kind of chance, then at some point we must stop bringing up his past at every opportunity.' He admitted that 'the Peters problem' had been 'a constant embarrassment', but argued that if a divinity faculty could not give such a man a chance, then he had no possibility at all of making good. 'I am quite sure that the old impudent impostures are behind him.'

Trevor-Roper expressed conditional agreement:

> if he is reformed, and if he really has some intellectual quality, then he should not be prevented by his past from obtaining suitable employment ... That indeed is the whole problem. I did think, at one time, that this might be so; and so I went as far as I decently could in his support when he applied for an archivist's job in Grimsby. But of course one cannot deceive employers. Now the position is that he is aiming higher again ...

He referred to the suspicion that Marie Peters had written

Oculus Episcopi: 'there is also the fact that he was notorious borrower of other people's theses in Oxford':

> If only one could feel sure that the work was genuine, and
> had some modest quality, then I feel that he might be allowed
> to slip into some suitably modest position; but I feel that, in
> fairness to possible employers, it is essential to be certain on
> this point ... If only he could be persuaded not to apply for
> academic posts, how much simpler it would be!

'I am afraid that he is only suited for a minor kind of academic post, perhaps in the realm of archiving,' replied Rupp. 'I regard him as a II (ii) mind and do not expect from him anything in the way of glowing or original scholarship.' He did not think that Mrs Peters had written *Oculus Episcopi* – if she had done, 'it would I think be much better than it is'. But, wrote Rupp, 'I believe his criminal past is behind him':

> I am well aware, and this is the tragic thing, that there are
> elements of instability in his character. It seems that of
> all worlds the academic is the hardest for an 'old lag' to
> rehabilitate himself in and the only thing I think we can do is
> to give what help we can, bearing in mind the real facts. I am
> afraid that it is not always easy to disentangle the facts from the
> kind of academic gossip which circulates wherever a good story
> is to be had, but I think we owe him at least the attempt to do
> so.

Perhaps Peters had hinted that he might do something extreme if thwarted, because Rupp ended his letter by arguing that 'it would be tragic if he were driven to desperate devices after a long period of utter failure to secure any kind of satisfactory employment.'

Rupp's backing helped Peters secure a temporary job for the spring term of 1966 as an assistant master at The Leys School, Cambridge – then boys only. (Rupp was friendly with the chaplain there.) The Leys had been founded as a Methodist school and, though it was no longer exclusively so, it maintained a strong Christian ethos. 'I need not say that this is your first real break,' Rupp wrote to Peters. If he performed well at The Leys, he would emerge with a valuable testimonial, which should help him obtain more permanent and suitable employment in the future. Rupp warned Peters not to abuse this opportunity, as he did not think there would easily be another. 'The thing is to study to be quiet and do your business, as the Bible says, and not to draw attention to yourself in any way, and certainly not to wear clerical collars or to engage in clerical activities.'

It looked as though Peters's problems might be over. Thanks to Rupp, he now had a degree, and a job – albeit a temporary one: perhaps the first step towards re-establishing himself in a legitimate career.

SIX

In which the parson does some silly things

Peters seems to have followed Rupp's advice, at least while he was teaching at The Leys. 'I understand that he did quite a good job there,' Bruce Lockhart informed Trevor-Roper once the term was over, following a conversation with W. A. (Alan) Barker, the headmaster. He felt that in a boys' school, so long as the headmaster was 'in the picture', Peters could not do much harm; and he himself would not go out of his way to prevent Peters from finding employment in the future – except in schools where girls were present.

Peters appeared in Oxford for the 1966 annual conference of the Catholic Record Society, publishers of the journal *Recusant History*. Most of the participants were Roman Catholics, and as the few Anglicans waited for them to emerge from Mass, Peters commented that perhaps they were late because they were saying matins from the Book of Common Prayer. Such a quip – paradoxically suggesting that Catholics should use the Anglican liturgy – suited the 'new ecumenism' then prevalent following the Second Vatican Council, which had revised the Catholic liturgy in a manner that offered hope of reconciliation between the Christian Churches. In the same spirit Peters agreed to preach a special service in the Roman Catholic Church in Tarporley in Cheshire, at the request of the parish priest, Father John Marmion, a regular attendee at the conferences. Peters also befriended William Price, then a postgraduate student, and invited the young man to visit him at home, where, he said, he kept a private oratory. Price saw no reason to doubt that Peters was as he presented himself, a scholarly Anglican priest; or that the woman he introduced as 'Mrs Peters' was his wife, as perhaps she was. So Price would be startled when, about two years later, the Assistant County Archivist at Shropshire Record Office remarked that 'Parson Peters' was notorious, and that archivists had been advised to watch him closely.

That summer, Rupp felt able to recommend Peters for a post as tutorial assistant in divinity at St Mary's College, part of the University of St Andrews. 'I think he has now established some sort of claim to have his past forgotten,' wrote Rupp in his reference, 'and to be taken on the merits of his performance in the last four years, which has shown a continuing maturing both in his character and in his teaching abilities.'

But before St Andrews could complete its deliberations Peters disappeared, leaving no forwarding address – which was perhaps just as well, for he was £357 in arrears on the rent for his Cambridge flat and had already been threatened with legal action. (The debt was written off.) In addition, he left numerous unpaid bills from Cambridge tradesmen, including one described as 'gigantic' from the booksellers Bowes and Bowes.*

---

* Some years later, at a dinner to launch a book in Manchester, Peters found himself seated next to the manager of Bowes and Bowes, who had not forgotten the gigantic bill. Peters extracted himself from this difficulty with

In fact he had bolted to America. He had obtained an assistant professorship at Hope College, Michigan, where he took up his post in September 1966. Just before leaving England, he married the sixth Mrs Peters, a Miss Ann Brinded, who followed him across the Atlantic, bringing with her his large and impressive collection of books, many of them of course acquired on credit and unpaid for.

Peters had been appointed in a hurry, after another man had accepted the job and then withdrawn at the last minute. Because of the rush, the normal procedures were not followed. Dr Paul G. Fried, chairman of Hope's history department, had interviewed Peters over a Coca-Cola at Heathrow Airport, while between flights; and had been so impressed that he had offered him the job without taking up his references.

Trevor-Roper first learned of Peters's second coming in America early in 1967, when he received a letter, asking what he knew of the character and background of a Mr Robert Peters, who had applied for a post at the University of Wisconsin-Milwaukee. Peters's credentials were impressive: a first in theology from Oxford, taken in 1953, followed by a B.Litt. in history. He had told the selection board at Wisconsin that he had been a research fellow and supervisor at Pembroke College, Cambridge; but he had given up his fellowship, as he held a pessimistic view of the prospects for further academic openings in England 'owing to the cutbacks by the Labour Government'. His application to Wisconsin was supported by a very favourable reference from the Dean of Pembroke, which Peters had

---

a plea of *non compos mentis*, arguing that no sane person would have run up such an account.

Robert Peters in 1966 or 1967, during his short-lived appointment
as assistant professor at Hope College, Michigan.

helpfully forwarded himself, as well as testimonials from Rupp
and the headmaster of The Leys. Though still in his first term he
wanted to abandon Hope, he said, as he was not satisfied with its
intellectual standard. (It would later transpire that he had been
so vocal in his criticisms that the irritated Hope authorities had
decided to dispense with his services at the end of the academic
year.)

The writer of the letter was a professor of history at Wisconsin, James A. Brundage, who had connections in Cambridge,

having spent some time there in the past. He was a witty, sophisticated correspondent, and Trevor-Roper enjoyed their exchanges, which would continue over the next few years. Brundage explained that Peters had come to Milwaukee and made a favourable impression on him and his colleagues, but as a matter of routine he had thought it necessary to investigate Peters's background before offering him a job. His enquiries at Pembroke had revealed that Peters was quite unknown there; Rupp had provided a bland response, but Geoffrey Elton had given a stern warning that Peters was a fraud, and had strongly urged Brundage to contact Trevor-Roper for more detail. Once Elton's letter had been received, there was no longer any question of Peters coming to Wisconsin.

Elton's attitude to Peters had hardened since the time, five years before, when he had reviewed *Oculus Episcopi* with lukewarm enthusiasm. A letter to Trevor-Roper in the dossier provided some explanation of his change of tune. 'I know how instrumental you have been in exposing this abominable fraud,' he would write in 1969. 'I've taken a small hand, too, because I ran into his trouble-making here [Cambridge] when he practised some particularly nasty bilking of tradesmen and unpleasantly pestered (socially, not sexually) some nice young people I know.'

Peters was not going to Milwaukee; but, as Trevor-Roper remarked in a letter to Dean Simpson, 'America is a large country.' As one door closed, several more swung temptingly ajar. Peters was offered a tenured position as an associate professor at the University of Texas. Nor was this all: he had been appointed to teach Renaissance and Reformation studies at the Catholic University of America in Washington. Small wonder that he would tell the police that he 'loved' America, 'because of the opportunities it offered'. Indeed, as the twentieth century progressed, the well-endowed universities of America would seem increasingly attractive to British academics, faced with cuts to their funding. At home there was fierce competition for any vacant post, whereas it appeared that jobs were plentiful on the other side of the Atlantic. In America, too, you could be anything that you wanted to be, provided that you had the qualifications, and Peters had plenty of those.

'I thought that I would never be surprised by anything Peters did,' Trevor-Roper replied to Brundage, though he admitted to being surprised in one respect. 'It is clear that Peters, for some obscure psychological reason, needs hierarchical ritualism. In Oxford he officiated (when he could) in an extremely ritualistic church, and when he married his nth wife in Marylebone he insisted (as the clergyman told me) on a nuptial mass.' So he thought it odd that Peters should now be teaching in Hope, which Brundage described as 'an obscure Calvinistic institution', even if he was only using it as a stepping stone to a more congenial location.

In his next curriculum vitae Peters's qualifications became still more impressive: as well as his first in theology from Oxford and of course his legitimate MA from Manchester, he was now boasting a first in history from Liverpool University, taken in 1951, MAs from both Oxford and Cambridge, and a Ph.D. from Manchester. On the strength of these and the testimonials already mentioned, Peters was offered a post by American University, which, like the Catholic University of America, was based in Washington, but affiliated to the Methodist Church. However, the offer was put on hold following a warning from the American Historical Association, alerted by Professor Brundage to the possibility that Peters might be claiming degrees that he did not in fact possess. Asked for an explanation, Peters responded that it was the result of 'a series of ghastly errors'; he was writing immediately to England to get the matter cleared up. To Brundage, the chairman of the history department at American University tentatively advanced the theory that there were two Robert Peters in this world, 'one making life hard for the other'.

American University sought clarification from Rupp, who confessed himself 'very distressed' at the situation: 'it really is an affront to academic honour that he should go on in this manner.' Rupp wrote to remonstrate with Peters himself: 'You seem to be doing silly things again and I do appeal to you rather desperately to stop it.' He warned that 'you are heading for disaster if you start this entirely stupid business again.'

To Brundage, Trevor-Roper expressed the view that the 'asinine' Rupp 'simply will not face facts, and out of misguided Christian charity is in fact unwittingly encouraging Peters to impose on innocent universities'. Brundage agreed that Rupp's part in 'the Peters business' showed no credit to his judgement or good sense. 'I can only assume that he must be a remarkably unworldly person':

> In his letter to the authorities at American University, Rupp protested that every word of the testimonial which he had written to me was true – and so it was, I suppose, in the sense that there was no overt *professio falsi* [dishonesty]; but *suppressio veri* [suppression of the truth] there was in abundance, and any ecclesiastical historian, I should have thought, ought to be a sufficiently nimble theologian to grasp that both categories are species of falsehood.

'A fig for the sanctimonious Rupp!' exclaimed Trevor-Roper in his reply to Brundage. 'Of the two of them, I vastly prefer Peters.'

Could we not let him nestle for a time in some cosy clerical chair – not at Oxford, of course, nor at Milwaukee – but in some solemn, high-minded institution whose subsequent loss of face we can bear with equanimity? I have no doubt that he will give lectures which will be no less stimulating, and perhaps no more erroneous, than many you and I have heard and safely forgotten. He will divert the Faculty with intimate personal gossip about academic life in places he has never seen ... Altogether, the appointment will add to the gaiety of nations, and who will suffer?

I think I shall write to Rupp a letter full of Christian contrition, saying that I have taken his reproof to heart, and that now, after long bouts of introspection, I have decided that he has been right all along about Peters, and I wrong, and that I now withdraw all my reservations ...

Tongue-in-cheek, Brundage suggested that Peters should find work as an academic administrator:

At least on this side of the ocean, deans, chancellors, vice-chancellors, provosts and the like frequently behave very much like con men. Perhaps you might suggest to the distinguished Rupp that his most famous pupil has missed a highly suitable outlet for his abilities.

He had discovered that Peters had narrowly missed being appointed Visiting Professor at the University of Illinois. A colleague involved in the selection of candidates for the post at Wisconsin, with whom Brundage had shared what he had learned about Peters from Trevor-Roper and others, discreetly mentioned the matter in a letter to a friend of his at Illinois. The friend, thinking this too ripe a tale not to repeat, shared it with a senior member of the history department; whereupon his senior colleague exclaimed, 'My God! That's the man we've just hired!' Fortunately, the letter of offer, though written, signed and sealed inside an envelope addressed to Peters, had not yet been sent and could be retrieved from the mailroom before it was dispatched: 'thus Peters was foiled once more.'

But it would have been too late for Peters even if the offer had been received, because he was on his way out of the country: he had been arrested by the FBI, and locked up in Wayne County jail, Detroit, where he was held for a few days, before being deported. After only six months' stay in America, he was once again being sent home. The grounds for deporting him were twofold: (a) he had failed to notify the US authorities of his 1953 deportation before his arrival; (b) he had falsified his age on his visa papers.

The case attracted coverage on national newscasts and several network television shows. The British consul was quoted as saying 'There is a slight kink in the man. He is not a dangerous man, but he is not altogether balanced.' The American media relished the piquant detail that a professor teaching college students was himself not in possession of a college degree. Hope College's embarrassed president, Dr Calvin A. VanderWerf, felt obliged to issue a statement of explanation. 'He came to us highly recommended and his papers were in apparent good order,' the President declared. 'We were greatly surprised to hear

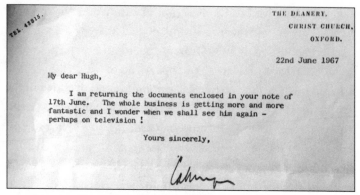

TEL. 48815.

THE DEANERY,
CHRIST CHURCH,
OXFORD.

22nd June 1967

My dear Hugh,

I am returning the documents enclosed in your note of
17th June. The whole business is getting more and more
fantastic and I wonder when we shall see him again –
perhaps on television !

Yours sincerely,

A note to Trevor-Roper from Cuthbert Simpson, Dean of Christ
Church. Simpson's prediction proved prescient – see pp. 151–3.

of his present difficulties.' To the Hope College magazine *The
Anchor*, he insisted that Peters had come with 'glowing credentials' and had been hired 'in good faith'. Poor Dr Fried, who had
interviewed Peters at Heathrow Airport, became known on the
Hope College campus as 'Dr Fraud'. In a letter to Trevor-Roper,
Brundage expressed his sympathy for Fried: 'At least he has the
consolation of knowing that the officers of a great many more
distinguished institutions than Hope College have made precisely the same mistake.'

For some months afterwards there was no sign of Peters. Trevor-
Roper thought it possible that he had gone to ground in Wales,
practising on innocent clergymen; or that he had reverted to
schoolteaching, 'probably in a girls' school'. Then, in July 1967,
Brundage received from Peters an offprint of an article that he
had written for an obscure learned journal – 'an intellectual
lightweight,' commented Brundage in a letter to Trevor-Roper,

'but not half so piffling as another recent paper of his'. The packet in which it came had been postmarked Edinburgh. 'I guessed as much,' replied Trevor-Roper, on hearing this. 'Scotland is the one constituent kingdom of the UK in which our old friend Robert Peters has not yet, as far as I know, operated in the academic world (though he has, of course, been in its police and magistrates' courts), so it seemed almost certain that he should remedy that defect.'

He wrote to warn the Bishop of Edinburgh that Peters was at large in his diocese. In a letter of thanks, the bishop revealed that Peters had appeared in the city two or three years before and had been in touch with him, 'after he had heard me preach a sermon which he said had greatly helped him.' The bishop was 'pretty certain' that he had not given Peters any money, 'though I may have given him lunch, and I think I wrote one or two letters about him to bishops in the south'. He admitted that he had believed Peters's story at the time, and that it had been not until some months afterwards that he had heard from a friend at least some of the true facts of the case.

From a fellow historian, Professor Denys Hay of Edinburgh University, Trevor-Roper learned that Peters had been teaching at Basil Paterson & Co., a posh local 'crammer', where he had been preparing students for sitting exams. However, when he applied for a post at George Watson's Ladies' College, a private day school in Edinburgh, Hay had recommended that his testimonials be investigated, with the result that Peters was once again 'blown'. Peters consulted Father Roland Walls, lecturer in divinity at New College, Edinburgh, and chaplain at Rosslyn Chapel, a few miles to the south of the city. Walls was a saintly man, founder of a religious community in a tin shack close to the chapel. He wrote to Rupp seeking advice on how to help Peters: 'I feel so helpless in this tangle.'

'I honestly don't know what the best thing to do about Robert Peters is,' replied Rupp. 'I think he behaves when there are people about who can keep an eye on him and know his history,' he argued – somewhat unconvincingly, given his own experiences. 'I am almost inclined to suggest that we form ourselves into a Society of the Friends of Robert Peters.' He proposed that the two of them might combine in writing to the Archbishop of Canterbury, in the hope that he would recommend an Anglican institution or library to take him. 'He has let us down so badly and so often that there is great difficulty in sponsoring him or writing any more recommendations for him, but from the Christian point of view we cannot let go of him now.' Otherwise, he feared, 'he will drift from one kind of folly to another and end up in prison or as a suicide'. But Rupp's indulgence went only so far: he declined to support Peters's application for a job as part-time history master at Croydon Grammar School.

'Nothing has happened to modify my firm and rational conviction that Rupp is an ass,' Trevor-Roper wrote to Brundage. Some months later he received another letter from Brundage, who had noticed an article about Erasmus (in whom Trevor-Roper had a special interest), in the periodical *Church History*, 'by Robert Peters, lecturer in history (part-time), Northwestern Polytechnic, London, England'. Since he had never heard of this institution, he asked Trevor-Roper to confirm its existence. 'I had not heard of it when I received your letter,' replied Trevor-Roper, 'but investigations have established its reality, and I suppose our old friend is objectively there too.'

As for his article in *Church History*, it only confirms my long held view that there is gross over employment and over production in our profession, and that half these periodicals could be painlessly suppressed without anyone suffering any harm whatsoever. Your account of Peters's article runs true to form: these niggling, trivial ejections which are particularly depressing when they are the result of sub-minds presuming to analyse the thought of real thinkers.

Trevor-Roper recommended Brundage to the most recent volume of the periodical *Studies in Church History*, where he would find 'a grave, judicious, portentous, condescending, trivial and trashy article by our old bogus friend, Robert Peters'.*

It is difficult to trace Peters's movements around this time, though one can catch an occasional glimpse of him. In March 1968, for example, the new President of Magdalen wrote a cautionary letter to the Secretary of the Oxford and Cambridge Club in Pall Mall, after seeing Peters's name in the candidates' book. In June Trevor-Roper received a handwritten note from the Dean of Christ Church, Cuthbert Simpson. He attached a postcard from 'your Canadian opposite number on the Peters saga', the Reverend Eugene Fairweather, who, during a visit to London, had spotted a notice in *The Times*, advertising a sermon to be preached by 'The Rev. Robert Peters' at St Paul's, Covent Garden. 'Is this our boy again?' asked Fairweather.†

As Trevor-Roper would soon discover, Peters was about to

---

* 'The notion of "the Church" in the writings ascribed to King James VI & I', *Studies in Church History*, 3.
† Peters had preached at St Paul's on another occasion four weeks earlier.

open a new front: scholarly publishing, a natural extension of his academic work. He had applied for a post, and been accepted, as an editor with Gregg International, publishers of scholarly reprints, based in Farnborough, Hampshire. The first that Trevor-Roper knew of this was when Geoffrey Elton forwarded to him a photocopied entry from the reputable newsletter 'Historians of Modern Europe'. The entry was for Robert Peters, who described himself, *inter alia*, as 'Consultant and Contributing Editor' for Gregg International Publishers, and 'General Editor of a series of Reformation Studies and 17th century Theology reprints, with new introductions and annotations'. These, of course, would be written by Peters. In this capacity he had applied, and been accepted, to read texts from the early modern period at the Bodleian Library. Trevor-Roper alerted Bodley's Librarian to the presence of a viper in his bosom.

In the dossier is a letter from the chief editor, giving an account of Peters's career at Gregg International. He had been due to begin on 1 August 1968, but 'a sudden operation' had delayed this starting date until 1 October. Peters had come into the office for two days and was then absent because of further ill-health until 21 October. In a subsequent interview with the managing director it had become apparent that, in the interval that had elapsed between his appointment and his actual commencement, Peters had completely altered his view of the nature of his duties, to a much higher level. He now saw himself in the role of a publishing director, rather than as a mere editor. Peters had offered to resign his more lowly position. The publishers said that they would be happy to consider any suggestions that he might care to submit for a publishing programme, which would then be considered and evaluated in the normal way. If the company decided to proceed, payment would be by results. 'There then ensued reams of paper, and in the end a request for payment on an hourly basis. When we refused to comply with his request we received several really offensive letters and finally a letter from his solicitors.' Peters continued to press the publishers for payment until the following August, when they told him politely but firmly that any further allegations would result in the strongest possible action by their own lawyers.

Peters's entry in 'Historians of Modern Europe' had indicated that he was now affiliated to the Institute of Social Anthropology, Oxford. Seeing this, Lucy Sutherland (now Dame Lucy Sutherland) was outraged. 'This really is intolerable,' she wrote to Trevor-Roper. 'Is Peters at this Institute of Social Anthropology now? And if so, can he be there without a college connection?'

She was right to ask the question, because in the Oxford system nobody could be a member of the university who was not also on the books of one of the colleges. Trevor-Roper made some enquiries and discovered that Peters had indeed arrived at the Institute, where he had applied to read for a diploma. 'He seems to have spun a very plausible and touching hard-luck story to the Secretary of the Institute, who is full of sympathy for his misfortunes,' Trevor-Roper reported. 'He was told that he must belong to a college, and (undeterred by previous experiences here) set off for Linacre' – then a new college, for graduates only, far less prestigious than Magdalen. 'I am told that he nearly succeeded there.' Peters had already written to the President of Magdalen requesting an interview. He referred to 'the attempts I am making to seek to re-establish myself in Oxford', and raised the possibility that he might be readmitted to Magdalen to enable him to study for a Diploma in Social Anthropology: 'The immediate purpose of my reading for this Diploma is to enhance my suitability for a post in an African university.' The President had declined to see him.

Six more months passed and then, in the summer of 1969, Trevor-Roper received a confidential letter from an old friend at Oxford University Press. He had been warned about Robert Peters, who was now working for OUP part-time (after applying unsuccessfully for a full-time job) as a copy editor. The writer asked Trevor-Roper if there was any risk in his being employed there.

Trevor-Roper provided a cautious endorsement. 'I would like to hear that Peters was settled in the kind of job that he can do,' he replied, 'and I think that copy editing is such a job.' But a week later he learned for the first time that Peters was working for a Ph.D. at Manchester. He outlined his concerns in a letter to Henry Chadwick, Regius Professor of Divinity and one of the academic 'Delegates' who oversee the governance of OUP. The Clarendon Press, the section in which Peters was working, received the pick of Ph.D. theses for possible publication. There were grounds for suspecting that Peters had been guilty of plagiarism in the past, and might be so in the future. 'I cannot exclude the possibility that one of the documents which passes through his hands as a copy editor may end up as part of his thesis for the Manchester Ph.D.'

His recommendation that Peters be barred from reading unpublished theses was adopted. Alas, these precautions were unavailing. The temptation proved too great: Peters was discovered secretly enjoying the forbidden fruit, and so expelled from that temporary Garden of Eden. 'I have been able to rid the Press of this troublesome (though erstwhile) priest,' Trevor-Roper's friend at OUP wrote to him.

Peters was still masquerading as an Anglican clergyman. He had some writing paper run up, headed 'THE REVD. R. P. PETERS'. One of his characteristics was to express indignation when his past conduct was questioned. This was evident in a furious letter that he wrote to the Reverend Mr Hope, vicar of St Michael's, New Marston (a suburb of Oxford), where Peters had officiated on several occasions. (Hope was a German whose original name was Hopf; perhaps Peters had thought that he might not be fully acquainted with the rules of the Church of England.) This letter was a reply to one from the embarrassed Hope, who had been instructed by the diocesan authorities that Peters should desist forthwith. A copy found its way into Trevor-Roper's dossier, via Henry Chadwick.

Peters had officiated at St Michael's 'only' (so he wrote to Hope) 'at your earnest entreaty'. He referred to 'the information you conveyed to me yesterday regarding the unsavoury gossip which unemployed minds apparently delight to indulge in, and to communicate to their like'. He was withdrawing his offer to preach at the forthcoming patronal festival: 'I have no wish to involve myself in ecclesiastical gossip, nor to contribute to it.' He had 'neither the time, patience, liking or energy to spare' from the purposes which had brought him to Oxford. By this stage in the letter he had worked himself into such a rage as to be barely coherent:

> Presumably, gossip has always found a breeding ground in any 'enclosed' community: equally presumably, it will always persist in such communities. That is unavoidable. What is avoidable is

participation in it; whether for one's own gratification, or as a source of fuel for the gratification of others.

He ended with cold formality:

With kindest possible regards to Mrs Hope and yourself, in which my wife joins,

I am,

Yours sincerely,

R. P. Peters

SEVEN

In which the parson appoints himself principal

'It is impossible to keep a good man down,' Trevor-Roper wrote to Brundage early in 1970, in a bulletin summarising Peters's most recent escapades: 'he soon bounces up again.' Peters had recently applied for the Chair of Social and Cultural History at the University of Malaya, Kuala Lumpur. 'Peters should not even be considered,' the academic assessor, Professor C. R. Boxer of Yale, had written, 'since he has a criminal record extending from Canada to Coromandel.' Boxer forwarded Peters's application form, the usual blend of fact and invention, to Trevor-Roper, with a covering comment: 'There is something rather engaging about the way in which he pursues his career of fraud and deceit without the slightest regard for occasional setbacks.'

Poor Peters was about to experience yet another setback. After six years, he had at last completed his Ph.D. thesis on 'King James VI and I as a Theologian'. Unfortunately for him, Rupp had by this time left Manchester for Cambridge, so it was submitted to his successor, the Reverend Professor Basil Hall. The external examiner, a professor from St Andrews, was puzzled by the thesis, which seemed chaotic, with an alarming number of inaccuracies in the citations, considerable confusion over the titles and contents of important contemporary documents, and long appendices of original material from the early seventeenth century without any critical apparatus or obvious relation to the main argument of the work. More important, the thesis failed to grapple with the fundamental issues raised. Professor Hall, who was wary of Peters after reading the file on him left by Rupp, took unusual precautions: on arriving for the oral, the external examiner was surprised to find himself flanked on either side, by the university's Assistant Registrar and by a solicitor. He was even more surprised to find the candidate unfamiliar with much of the content of his own thesis. In the circumstances, he could hardly award him a Ph.D. The result was a fail.

Peters telephoned Hall and complained that the decision was unjust. Several scholars in Oxford had praised his thesis, including Henry Chadwick (the newly appointed Dean of Christ Church, in succession to Cuthbert Simpson). Hall wrote to Chadwick: was it true that he had seen Peters's thesis and thought well of it? Because both the internal and external examiners had found little to praise and much to criticise. Chadwick's reply, which he copied to Trevor-Roper, was reassuring: 'I hardly know Mr R. P. Peters, and have at no time either seen his thesis or discussed its subject matter with him.'

Never one to surrender until he had exhausted his ammunition, Peters appealed to the Vice-Chancellor, Sir William Mansfield Cooper, suggesting that he should resubmit the thesis with revisions; or, failing that, should be allowed to return to Manchester to pursue a fresh thesis on a different topic. Sir William saw no grounds for acceding to either of his requests. Peters tried again, hinting that unfair prejudice had influenced the decision to fail him. Sir William replied that he had nothing to add to what he had already written. By this time Peters had appealed to Her Majesty the Queen, in her capacity as the University of Manchester's Visitor. 'I left the examination with the firm impression that the thesis had been prejudged before the examination took place,' Peters informed her. He cited a letter from Rupp, who had read some chapters of the thesis and had incautiously told Peters that there was 'a great deal of new and useful stuff in it'. The monarch wisely decided not to become embroiled; she delegated the decision (as was her practice) to the Privy Council, which in turn referred the matter back to the Vice-Chancellor. The university took further legal advice, instructing Leon Brittan, the future Home Secretary, then a young barrister who had appeared for the University of London in a similar case three years earlier. Rupp prepared to support Peters and it was only with great difficulty that Hall persuaded him to back down, by pointing out that he would have to attend chambers in London and defend his judgement under cross-examination by counsel. Some years later, when he was due to leave Manchester, Professor Hall would photocopy part of the contents of the Peters file and forward the copies to Trevor-Roper.

While all this was going on Peters had not been idle, as Trevor-Roper discovered by chance when a former pupil of his was offered a post to teach history at the 'American International University' at Dropmore, a country house on the Thames near Beaconsfield. The post was vacant because they had suddenly dispensed with the previous incumbent, a Mr Robert Peters.

Peters had answered an advertisement in the *Times Higher Educational Supplement* to teach at this newly created campus for American students. He had arrived for his interview wearing a dog collar, claiming to hold a PhD in history; and given the impression towards his prospective employer that they would be lucky to have him. 'I know you're all right,' he reassured the college Principal, Dr Graddon Rowlands, 'because I've looked up your qualifications'. It did not then occur to Rowlands to do the same. Peters was hired to teach to teach medieval, and later modern, history; students found him condescending but otherwise satisfactory. In due course the Principal was invited to visit Peters at his house in Oxford, where he was introduced to Mrs Peters. He noticed the floor-to-ceiling shelves, bulging with books.

Peters continued to wear a dog collar, and carried a portable altar kit in the boot of his car so as to be ready to conduct a service at any time. When one of the students was killed in a motorbike accident, Peters offered to hold a memorial service at a nearby church; but the mourners indicated that they would prefer the local vicar. Peters was incandescent. 'I've never been so insulted in my life,' he raged. Uncertain how to handle this awkward situation, the Principal consulted the Bishop of Oxford, who advised that on no account should Peters be allowed to conduct a religious service. His suspicions raised, the Principal began to check Peters' references, most of which turned out to be bogus; one of his referees, the ecclesiastical historian W. H. C. Frend of Caius College, Cambridge, was seriously embarrassed to be approached. The Principal summoned Peters and dismissed him without further notice. Afterwards he received an angry telephone call from Mrs Peters. What he had done was 'totally unforgivable', she said, and it had made her husband 'seriously ill'; they were planning to sue for wrongful dismissal.

Dropped by Dropmore, Peters quickly found himself another

DEGREE OF DOCTOR OF PHILOSOPHY

Report on Thesis and Oral Examination of............ R.P. PETERS

Title of Thesis: King James VI & I as a Theologian.

Report on Thesis: (Note to Examiners: A joint report is preferred, but examiners are at liberty to submit separate reports or additional comments. It is a convenience if reports are typed. Please include comments both on the treatment of the subject and on its presentation.)

We cannot accept Mr. Peters' thesis as fulfilling the requirements for the Ph.D. Degree on the following grounds:
(1) He has failed to give a critical examination of the contents of the volume entitled Workes of James to ascertain the extent to which James was responsible for these writings. In view of the important article by D. H. Willson published in 1945, which is summarily dismissed by Mr. Peters, we feel that the question of the establishment of authorship and the critical analysis of the various editions of the separate and the collective works have not been dealt with properly by the candidate.
(2) We have noted a number of inaccuracies in his citations from both primary and secondary sources, sometimes in ways which affect the strength of his arguments.
(3) Mr. Peters showed considerable ignorance and confusion on the titles and contents of important contemporary documents essential to an understanding of James's early ecclesiological environment and the background to the development of his theological thinking.
(4) Moreover at the Oral Examination he admitted failure to take into account the depth of Scottish theological development in the last decades of the sixteenth century which forms the essential background to James's mature theological understanding and writings. (over)

(continue overleaf if necessary)

Report on Oral Examination:
We examined the candidate for an hour and forty minutes on the matters raised above and by his answers to our questions he showed beyond doubt his inability to grapple with the fundamental issues which were raised.

RECOMMENDATION (Please tick as appropriate and add comments if thought fit).

☐ 1. Award (no corrections needed).

☐ 2. Award and permit minor corrections.*

☐ 3. Award but insist on minor corrections.*

☑ 4. Reject (with no recommendation as to re-submission).

☐ 5. Reject but advise candidate to offer the thesis for a degree of Master.

☐ 6. Reject but permit submission of a revised thesis:

    (a) with/without further oral examination,

    (b) after further research as indicated.

* as listed or indicated on separate sheet attached.

The examiner's report on Peters's failed Ph.D., 1970.

position, this time in the new Open University, as full-time staff tutor in theology for the south-west region. He consulted Rupp as to whether it would be detrimental to his further career as an academic to pursue his appeal against Manchester's decision. In two long telephone calls, Hall persuaded Rupp to advise Peters that it would not be in his interests to continue. Early in October Peters wrote grandly to Sir William Mansfield Cooper to announce that he had withdrawn his petition because his circumstances had changed:

> I have been appointed to the staff of a British university and I consider that it would be most unseemly for a member of staff of one university to engage in dispute with another university.

The Open University's regional director for the south-west, R. H. Cosford, had not been asked to give an opinion on the appointment, which had been imposed upon him by the central office, influenced by Rupp. He had his doubts, having heard rumours about Peters from contacts at the Bodleian, and began making enquiries. Peters had claimed to hold a licentiate in theology from Durham, so Cosford wrote to Durham to check; the Registrar there could find no record of any man of that name possessing that particular qualification. Cosford also telephoned Trevor-Roper, who was able to identify several more mis-statements in Peters's application form. The accumulated evidence proved sufficient to send Peters on his way.

Trevor-Roper's Edinburgh informant Denys Hay wrote to tell him that, in the most recent newsletter issued by the Society for Renaissance Studies, he had noticed among its new members a 'Professor Robert Peters', giving an address in Walton Street,

Oxford. 'I at once experienced a strange creeping under the skin on the back of my neck,' wrote Hay, 'and I wondered if our old friend had made a re-appearance. He is such a plausible character that he might well get himself on to the committee of any body he was connected with.' Trevor-Roper confirmed that this was indeed the same Robert Peters and agreed that the Society's secretary should be warned against him. Perhaps Peters would do no harm – but he was not a man to be trusted, and the very presence of such a person on the committee tended to lower its scholarly standing.

In a letter from Wisconsin, Professor Brundage remarked to Trevor-Roper that Peters had been seen at an international congress of historians in Moscow in August. Among those attending was Emmet Larkin, a professor of history at the University of Chicago. Some years later, when Trevor-Roper was visiting Chicago, Larkin would give an account of his experience of Peters in Moscow. He had been invited, before the congress, to organise a discussion on the subject of the Roman Catholic Church in the English-speaking countries in the nineteenth century. He had arranged for six papers of half an hour each. On his arrival in Moscow he discovered that, by some manoeuvre which he did not understand, not he but Robert Peters, now apparently connected with 'the Catholic University in England', would be chairman of the discussion. Reluctantly he yielded the chair to Peters, who started to impose new rules, requiring all participants to reduce their papers to a précis. Larkin, an Irishman, was unwilling to take orders from an unknown Englishman: he declined to do so. After a long and acrimonious discussion, the matter was put to a vote and Peters was defeated. Afterwards Peters approached Larkin and said that he hoped there had been no 'misunderstanding'. Larkin, still fuming, told Peters that he had no interest in understanding him. Peters tried to obtain the text of the papers, but Larkin declined to surrender his. Trevor-Roper told him that he had been wise to refuse.

Also at the congress was Father Robert Trisco, of the Catholic University of America, with which Peters had been negotiating before he was deported from the United States three years before. Not having anything else to do, Trisco had agreed to join Peters for lunch in one of the university restaurants. Over the meal Peters told him that the Catholic University in England was in such dire financial straits that he had not received his monthly salary since the previous April, and that a planned summer session had been cancelled for lack of funds. While the teachers who had been brought in from outside had been placated with a certain amount, members of the faculty, who had expected to be able to supplement their income by giving a course or two, had received not a penny in compensation. Trisco suspected that he was being set up for a loan and steered the conversation on to safer subjects. He refrained from asking Peters how, if money was so short, he had been able to afford the trip to the Soviet Union.

Peters was hankering once again for the rich but prohibited pastures of the New World. At the Moscow congress he had proudly announced (though not to Trisco) that he was due to take up a position at Western University, Ontario. This was his third attempt to establish himself in Canada. Alas, the announcement was premature. Western University had interviewed him briefly in London, as Trevor-Roper learned subsequently from the professor of history there. The interviewer had sent a cable back to Canada 'satisfied', but another candidate was appointed instead. For some months Peters threatened to sue the university for breach of contract. He had been so confident of the job that he had applied for a permit to enter Canada and take up employment there. As a result, the university received a visit from the Royal Canadian Mounted Police, since it was suspected that the man who had applied for the permit might be the same Robert Peters who had been deported from Canada in the past, on being found to have a criminal record.

Peters's application to Western University had been supported not only by the familiar forged testimonial from Pembroke College, Cambridge, but by apparently authentic testimonials from Rupp and from Patrick Collinson, a specialist in the reign of Elizabeth I and another former pupil of Sir John Neale. Collinson, who had grown up in an intensely religious household, had considered becoming an Anglican priest himself before opting to become an historian. For the past decade he had taught at King's College, London, before, in 1969, taking up a post as Professor of History at the University of Sydney, Australia. He had previously supported Peters in a failed application to become Vice-Principal of one of the colleges in the University of Durham, saying that he thought him 'well-qualified' for the post. 'But for a very unorthodox past, a man of his years and quality would hold a prominent post,' Collinson had stated.

Trevor-Roper was somewhat surprised by this, since he liked Collinson and thought highly of him. He sent Collinson a copy of the testimonial, querying whether it was genuine. In reply, Collinson acknowledged that he had acted as a referee for Peters on numerous occasions, so frequently that he had provided him with an open testimonial. It had been his custom, when acting as a referee, to discuss rather frankly certain aspects of Peters's past, so as to alert employers who might be unaware of these and so that he should not be thought to be supporting him in ignorance of the circumstances. He was therefore surprised, on seeing the copy of his open testimonial that Peters had submitted, to find that it did no more than hint at 'unusual problems' in Peters's past. Not having his own copy of the original, he could not be certain, but he did not exclude the possibility that Peters had omitted some parts of his original letter.

In justifying his support, Collinson sought to differentiate between Peters past and present:

> My honest impression of Peters in recent years, based upon
> sight of medical certificates, was that he had received successful
> psychiatric treatment for a condition, which went some way
> to explaining his fraudulent behaviour ... In writing references
> I was careful to speak of his record since the completion of
> the M.A. In recent years he has been a productive scholar, and
> I have seen something of what lies behind his publications
> when I have browsed his personal library (when visiting him in
> Oxford)* and have discussed matter of common interest with
> him. That he is nowadays (or was in 1968/9 when I last had
> contact with him) a relentless scholar, never out of the libraries,
> is no more in doubt than the fact that he practised widespread
> deception in the 1950s.

He added that he should be glad to know of any evidence that

---

* 'I am also greatly envious of his magnificent library,' Collinson wrote in one of the testimonials that he provided for Peters, perhaps unaware that many of the books had not been paid for.

Peters had continued to act fraudulently, or in any other way should have forfeited the right to consideration in respectable academic circles. When Trevor-Roper presented him with overwhelming proof to that effect, he repented: 'You leave me in no doubt that I have been taken for a ride.'

'Peters is a crook,' wrote Trevor-Roper. 'He is also, as everyone agrees, a very plausible crook, and, as I know, by direct experience, is wonderfully good at presenting a face of injured innocence.'

Since coming across Peters, Trevor-Roper had often contemplated writing a book about him. By now, more than a dozen years after his first encounter with the bogus parson, the dossier he had been keeping on 'our old friend' was a thick one. Peters's antics provided a source of repeated entertainment, exposing the gullibility of academic and religious institutions across the world. Trevor-Roper had become a connoisseur of fraud.

By chance, Trevor-Roper found himself writing about another extraordinary fraudster, after he was ceremoniously handed a parcel by a Swiss professor at Basel Airport one early August day in 1973. Inside was 'one of the most fascinating (and outrageous) documents I have ever read', the beautifully written but obscene memoirs of an eccentric English baronet who had died in 1944, after living most of his adult life in China. Sir Edmund Backhouse had been a respected Sinologist, the co-author of two influential books, based largely on Chinese sources, which had provided a unique picture of the last days of imperial rule. Between 1913 and 1921 he had donated to the Bodleian Library a magnificent collection of Chinese books and manuscripts; in recognition, his name had been inscribed on a marble tablet honouring the library's most generous benefactors. Backhouse's entry in the *Dictionary of National Biography* conveyed an impression of a shy scholar – but the memoirs revealed a hidden side to this reputable character. They showed that Backhouse had gone to Peking in the 1890s to enjoy the exquisite homosexual delights of Manchu decadence. Nor had he confined himself to these; at the age of thirty-one, he had become the lover of Tz'u-hsi, the Empress Dowager herself, she being then in her seventieth year.

Trevor-Roper relished the thought of presenting this pornographic memoir to the prudish (as he saw them) curators of the Bodleian and trying, with a grave face, to persuade them that it was their duty to publish it. The contrast with Backhouse's reputation as an unworldly, modest, bookish personality lent delicious piquancy to the story. But quite soon Trevor-Roper began to have doubts about Backhouse's veracity. His mind boggled at the discovery that such a character could have been elected to a chair in Chinese at King's College, London.* 'Do you think that perhaps Sir E. Backhouse may have imagined it all?' he asked a confidant. 'I am beginning to wonder.' He made discreet enquiries about Backhouse, though 'the more one seeks to find out about him, the more elusive he appears'. Within a few weeks his suspicions of the memoirs had hardened. He decided that nothing Backhouse had written could be relied upon. He therefore decided to build up Backhouse's history, as far as possible, solely from external sources. In the process, what had begun

---

* Backhouse did not take up the post, preferring to wait instead for the Oxford professorship, which in the event he never obtained. He had left Merton College, Oxford, almost twenty years before without taking a degree.

as an exercise to test the reliability of the memoirs became an adventure in biography.*

The archival sources he consulted strengthened Trevor-Roper's scepticism about the memoirs. But what they revealed was just as fascinating, and perhaps still more outrageous. Backhouse, the respected scholar, turned out to be a forger, a fraud, a charlatan of epic proportions – a con man who had bamboozled distinguished scholars and librarians, cynical journalists, hard-headed Scottish and American businessmen, senior diplomats, generals and politicians. He forged a memoir of a high Chinese official which he then used as a source, presented himself as a representative of the imperial court to negotiate deals to buy warships and print banknotes, claimed to have visited a male brothel with Henry James, boasted of a homosexual affair with the future prime minister Lord Rosebery, and much else. Trevor-Roper greeted each discovery with glee. Gradually he formed a picture of this elusive personality. He realised that Backhouse's behaviour could not be explained simply in terms of mercenary motives. Rather, like Peters, he was a fantasist, for whom the line between reality and lies had become blurred. Trevor-Roper speculated that Backhouse may have convinced himself of his own fabrications. His irresistible air of sincerity, which over-whelmed his victims' resistance, suggests as much. Moreover there was often, if not always, a small seed of fact in the stories that sprouted from his imagination.

Backhouse's astounding career, as revealed by Trevor-Roper,

----

* Trevor-Roper's book about Backhouse, *A Hidden Life*, was published in 1976; the American edition, renamed *Hermit of Peking*, came out the following year.

invited comparison with another great fantasist, Frederick Rolfe, the self-styled 'Baron Corvo'. Inevitably, too, Trevor-Roper was reminded of 'the Reverend' Robert Peters.

In the early 1970s Peters had become a lecturer at the Bible Institute, Birmingham, a Charismatic Christian training college, after the Principal, Brash Bonsall, struggling with a staffing crisis, had urged his flock to pray for help from the Almighty. When Peters arrived unannounced, he was greeted as the answer to their prayers.

Perhaps teaching at the Bible Institute inspired Peters to set up his own establishment, because in 1973 he suddenly emerged as Principal of 'St Aidan's College', which described itself as 'an ecumenical centre for religious studies'. This new institution was housed in a redundant rectory, surrounded by woods and farmland, in the small Shropshire village of Willey. Named after the great Celtic missionary, St Aidan's, Salop, could be confused by the unwary with Peters's own alma mater, St Aidan's, Birkenhead, which had only recently closed; or with St Aidan's, a college within the University of Durham. The prospectus issued by this St Aidan's offered several courses of study, including full-time residential courses (the college had three student bedrooms), weekend residential courses and correspondence courses: preparing students for such qualifications as the Diploma in Theology or a Bachelor of Divinity, both accredited by the University of London, or for St Aidan's own college certificate. Negotiations were under way with other accreditation boards. The college also offered 'ecumenical retreats' and 'study conferences'. A circular letter sent to 2,500 heads of religious education departments in schools outlined the services offered

St Aidan's Theological College, Shropshire.

The Principal officiates at a service.

by the college and promised respondents the personal attention of the Principal. Though he did not advertise this fact, Peters took almost all the classes himself, as the sole in-house tutor.

The college had three trustees: the Principal himself, Mrs Peters (the 'Lady Warden') and a Mr Drury, apparently some form of accountant. A fourth trustee, an Anglican vicar from Devon, resigned on receiving information about the Principal from his local archdeacon. The Principal acted as 'Father Confessor' as well as tutor; the Lady Warden as secretary, bursar, altar server and cook.

The prospectus stressed that liturgical worship was 'central to the life and work of the college'. The Eucharist was celebrated daily, a period of meditation was observed at midday and there were evening prayers at 7.00 p.m. 'The Liturgy is compiled from Taizé,* new Roman and other modern rites, with a litany from the Liturgy of St John Chrysostom.' This was pretty recherché for the average Anglican, an indication of Peters's love of ritual. According to the brochure, the liturgy was designed to allow for flexibility, 'as befits the worship of a College committed to deepening understanding among Christians of different traditions'. Peters, who officiated at all the services, now took to wearing a cassock and a dog collar at all times. An academic gown hung prominently in his study; the Principal was considering a rule to compel students to wear gowns in class. The day was strictly timetabled, from 7.30 in the morning until 9.45 at night; a group of students who made a late-evening exodus to the nearest pub

---

* The Taizé community is an ecumenical monastic order in Burgundy. Its services consist of distinctive and much-repeated prayer chants, interspersed with periods of meditative silence.

was very severely reprimanded. A notice in each of the bedrooms instructed students that Peters was to be addressed at all times as 'Principal' or 'Father', not as 'Mr' and never as 'Reverend'. Thus at one stroke he had achieved the status, both sacerdotal and professorial, for which he had yearned so long.*

Peters was leading a double life. As well as acting as Principal of St Aidan's, he was working as a schoolteacher, perhaps to earn enough to pay his way, because St Aidan's was never a money-spinner. Under the name Robert Parkins he accepted a post as head of religious education at Aylestone School in Hereford, about fifty miles away. For a while he juggled these two roles, keeping them separate long enough for him to woo and win the hand of a colleague, the head of the lower school, who became his sixth or probably seventh wife – apparently unaware that under the name Peters he had another wife in Shropshire, who perhaps was just as unaware that she had been supplanted. Sadly, Parkins had to give up teaching at Aylestone when it became known that he had lied about his qualifications. His seventh marriage seems to have lasted no longer than his third.

In September 1974 St Aidan's came to the attention of the Regius Professor of Divinity at Cambridge, Geoffrey Lampe. Though an Anglican priest and theologian, Lampe was no milk-and-water Christian: during the Second World War, while serving as chaplain to 34 Armoured Brigade, he had been

---

* Two years later, on 20 March 1976, friends were invited to attend the ceremony (followed by a buffet lunch) of Peters's commissioning as 'vicar forane' of the Old Catholic Church – defined as an experienced priest appointed by a bishop to exercise limited jurisdiction over a specific part of a diocese.

awarded the Military Cross for his courage in rescuing wounded troops under enemy fire. As Regius Professor, he was chairman of the committee which authorised courses in religious knowledge for the Cambridge Local Examination Board. In 1973 his committee had acceded to a request from the Principal of St Aidan's for its recognition as a centre for such examinations, on the strength of the college's prospectus and of a letter from the Principal, which had stated (falsely, as it turned out) that the college had been recognised by the University of London. Since then Lampe had received a disquieting report from a clergyman who had attended (incognito) a short vacation course at St Aidan's on 'the phenomenology of religion and contemporary theologians'. As it turned out, there were only six students present. Except for a lecture given by a visiting Catholic priest, the teaching was entirely carried out by Peters, and was described in the clergyman's report as 'ludicrously incompetent'. Classes consisted of gross generalisations, liberal peppering of impressive-sounding names and vitriolic attacks on other scholars. Anyone who questioned anything that Peters said was accused of being a troublemaker.

Lampe made further enquiries, beginning with the Bishop of Hereford, in whose diocese the college was situated. The bishop's reply was blunt: 'The Principal is an impostor, and his college is completely bogus.' The bishop referred him to David Carey, the archbishop's chief legal adviser, who was even more damning: 'Peters is the biggest crook on the Archbishop's blacklist of misbehaving clergymen.' (In 1975 Carey would make a representation to the Home Secretary on behalf of the General Synod, asking for Peters to be exempted from a condition of the new Rehabilitation of Offenders Act, which stipulated that criminal records should not be disclosed to potential employers.) With his letter to Lampe, Carey attached the memorandum about Peters written in 1954 by the then Archbishop of Canterbury, Geoffrey Fisher, which contained some interesting details of Peters's early career. He had first come to the archbishop's notice in 1945, as a newly 'inhibited' priest. Even then he was already claiming to have a degree from the University of Liverpool, a claim supported by a forged letter from the Vice-Chancellor. Over the next few years, as well as repeatedly forging academic testimonials for himself, Peters had gone so far as to falsify his letters of orders.

Lampe consulted Rupp, now near at hand as Dixie Professor of Ecclesiastical History at Cambridge, who provided a summary of his dealings with Peters and said that he had seen nothing of him for the past three or four years. He warned that Peters was liable to turn vicious when rumbled. Lampe also approached Trevor-Roper, who replied that he was 'always fascinated' to hear of Peters's latest adventures: 'It is true, I have a very large file on Peters, full of detail; but not if I had a hundred tongues and a voice of brass* could I recount all the twists and turns of his life that have come to my notice.' With his reply Trevor-Roper enclosed a digest of all that he had discovered about Peters. This convinced Lampe, if he were not already convinced, that St Aidan's was 'wholly undesirable on ecclesiastical, educational

---

* 'Had I a hundred mouths, a hundred tongues,
A voice of brass, and adamantine lungs,
Not half the mighty scene could I disclose,
Repeat their crimes, or count their dreadful woes!'
Virgil, *Aeneid*, VI, 890–94.

and personal grounds'. He speedily ensured that the Cambridge Local Examination Board withdrew its recognition of the college as an examination centre – prompting a succession of protests, accusations of malice and threats of legal action from the Principal. 'I don't want to persecute an unfortunate man,' Lampe wrote to Canon Robert Holtby, General Secretary of the National Society for Promoting Religious Education, 'but I am very anxious indeed to discourage a bogus educational establishment.'

The Secretary to the Cambridge Local Examination Board received several indignant letters of complaint about its decision to withdraw recognition of St Aidan's, from someone claiming to be a student there, a Miss A. Brinded – coincidentally the maiden name of the Lady Warden. Peters was outraged when, at Lampe's urging, a letter was sent to Chief Education Officers around the country, warning them not to allow public money to be wasted in grants to students to pay for them to attend courses at St Aidan's. When Christian publications such as the *Church Times* began to refuse his advertisements, Peters wrote irate letters to them demanding to know the reason. In fact St Aidan's had already come to the attention of the Church of England's Council on Foreign Relations (meaning relations with churches outside the Anglican Communion), which circulated a memorandum warning against two rogue *presbyteri vagantes* (wandering clergyman) – one being Peters and the other Roger Gleaves, the self-styled 'Bishop of Medway', who had been convicted of serious sexual offences against adolescent boys and, like Peters, claimed Old Catholic orders.

Time was running out for St Aidan's. In June 1975 a story appeared in the *Sunday People*, headed 'DEARLY BELOVED, PARSON PETERS IS A PHONEY'. 'A lot of people are paying good

DEARLY BELOVED, PARSON PETERS IS A PHONEY

By GRAHAM BALL

A LOT of people are paying good money for the pious words of the Rev. Robert Peters.

But verily we say unto you his reverence is a phoney.

True he was once a real Church of England parson. But he was unfrocked in 1953.

In the same year he was deported from America for illegally entering the country. Subsequently he served prison sentences, the last being in 1955.

Now the Reverend Peters is running his own centre of religious teaching.

He has made himself principal of St. Aidan's College at Willey in the heart of Shropshire.

More than 50 adult students are paying up to £150 a term for the religious instruction.

Worthless

Their reward at the end of the course: A St. Aidan's College certificate. Unhappily for the students it is worthless.

The Rev. Peters himself admits the certificate is not recognised.

"But," he said, "I have high hopes that in the next few years it will become established as a recognised theological qualification."

Still in a dog-collar ... Robert Peters, unfrocked 22 years ago.

Cutting from the *Sunday People*, 8 June 1975.

money for the pious words of the Rev. Robert Peters,' it began. 'But verily we say unto you, His Reverence is a phoney.' The story outlined Peters's record, before homing in on the college:

> Students are paying up to £150 a term for the Peters brand of religious instruction. Their reward at the end of the course: a St Aidan's College certificate. Unhappily for the students, it is worthless.

Peters himself admitted to the *Sunday People* reporters that the certificate was not 'at present' recognised but said, 'I have high hopes that in the next few years it will become established as a recognised theological qualification.' Asked about the warning letter sent out to all Chief Education Officers, he countered,

'People are apt to be wary of any new venture.' Questioned about his status as an unfrocked priest, Peters responded, 'I am not a practising minister. I call myself Reverend by right. I've been ordained.' When the reporters brought up his prison record, Peters lost his cool. 'This is preposterous,' he exploded. 'I am not prepared to answer. Leave this house immediately.'

There was an ironic coda to this story. Only a fortnight or so after the *Sunday People* exposé, a letter was published in the *Times Higher Education Supplement* complaining about institutions offering bogus qualifications. It was signed 'Robert Peters (Principal), St Aidan's College, Salop'.

EIGHT

In which the professor comes a cropper

Following his exposure in the *Sunday People*, Peters again disappears from Trevor-Roper's record. For a while the professor assumed that St Aidan's had collapsed in a cloud of bad debts; subsequently he discovered that, though wounded, the college had limped on for a while. In 1976, for example, schools received a mailing from St Aidan's offering summer courses for teachers of O- and A-levels in religious knowledge. The college may have survived for as long as another two years, because in his next curriculum vitae Peters would describe himself as 'Principal, St Aidan's College, Willey, Shropshire, 1973–8'. Indeed, his entry in *The Writers' Directory 1980–82* stated that he was still Principal of St Aidan's, giving the Shropshire address (presumably because its copy deadline had been some years before its publication date). Peters himself was described as a 'writer on ecclesiastical history', his works being four facsimile volumes published in the early 1970s by Scolar Press, as well as *Oculus Episcopi*. The *Writers' Directory* entry repeated the familiar claim that he had been 'Supvr. in English Studies, Pembroke Coll., Cambridge 1965–66' and added a new one, that he had been 'Temporary Lectr. in Sociology of Religion, Birmingham Univ., 1972–3'.

Trevor-Roper often entertained his friends with an account of Peters's misdeeds. While driving from Cambridge to Oxford, for example, he expatiated at length on the subject to his passenger Richard Cobb, who chortled as one outrageous act followed another. Cobb was especially amused by Peters's insistence on a nuptial mass during his third wedding; he imagined attending the next such ceremony and calling out, 'There *is* an impediment.' In a letter of thanks afterwards, Cobb likened Peters to Backhouse. 'I do feel,' he wrote, 'that he merits further study, perhaps even a short biography, as he is fairly outstanding both as an academic fraud and as a bigamist.'

A handwritten document headed 'Peters: notanda'* survives in Trevor-Roper's dossier:

Trevor-Roper identified in Peters a set of characteristics recognisable in others. In 1978, for example, he was reminded of Peters

---

* Latin for 'things to be noted'. Trevor-Roper was a classical scholar and his writings are peppered with Latin and Greek words and phrases.

when reading an article about a delinquent nineteenth-century clergyman, the Reverend J. G. Gibson, Rector of Ebchester. He sent a letter of praise to the article's author, a scholar in Durham. 'I have read it with fascination,' he wrote. 'It raises many questions, which I raise only rhetorically.' These questions culminated with the one he considered most significant: 'why on earth did he do it?' Had Gibson poured an equivalent amount of energy and ingenuity into legitimate pursuits, he would surely have achieved much. As with Gibson, so with Backhouse: the question was unanswerable in rational terms. 'You ask how many such characters there are,' he continued. 'I believe that they are legion.'* He mentioned 'one other who seems to me very similar to the Rev. J. G. Gibson: the Rev. Robert Peters, a bogus (or at least a defrocked) parson with a heroic career of imposture'. Among his many degrees, 'paraded only in the safety of the Antipodes', was B.Mus., Durham: 'if he comes your way please tell me.' Trevor-Roper explained that he was collecting information about Peters: 'Although I have a thick file on him, I can't publish anything. He would frighten publishers by threatening litigation.'

The dossier does not reveal what had aroused Trevor-Roper's fears of litigation (for defamation) if he published anything about Peters. Perhaps he had discussed the possibility with his editor or his literary agent, or both, and had been advised of the risks of writing about a living person. He was certainly no stranger to litigation. Plenty of people knew that Trevor-Roper was keeping a dossier on Peters. Perhaps Peters had become aware of this himself and had somehow indicated that he was ready to take action to defend his reputation; he had threatened to sue

---

* 'My name is Legion; for we are many.' Mark 5:9.

others in the past, and would do so in the future. In his trans-
actions with others, Peters would occasionally intimate, usually
with a suggestion of menace, that he had some legal training.

Following the collapse of St Aidan's and the failure of his
Ph.D. at Manchester, Peters was accepted by the Department of
Religious Studies in the University of Aberdeen to read for an
M.Litt. degree, later upgraded to a Ph.D. Gavin White's dossier
tells us that he married there, for a seventh or perhaps eighth
time, but alas, there are no further details and this marriage, too,
seems to have been short-lived – and of course was bigamous.
His supervisor in Aberdeen, the historian Dr Adrian Hastings,
might have been selected as someone likely to be sympathetic
to a person such as Peters – as perhaps he was, since Peters had
a keen eye for people's susceptibilities and knew how to exploit
them. Hastings was a Catholic priest, restless, energetic and
idiosyncratic; his determination to marry the woman he loved
(an Anglican at that), in defiance of Catholic teaching, set him
on a collision course with his church, causing his bishop to bar
him from ministering in public. The wedding in 1979 caused a
sensation, making the lead story on the front pages of tabloid
newspapers such as the *Sun* and the *Daily Express*. Peters, too,
could portray himself as a man of God cruelly blocked from
pursuing his vocation because of his love for a good woman
(or women) and persecuted by the gutter press. Hastings had
a special interest in African Christianity, and had spent much
of his early career teaching in East Africa; Peters professed an
interest in the African Church and offered as a topic for his
thesis 'Concepts and Patterns of Ministry in Some African Mis-
sions, Related and Independent Churches'. On this basis he was
accepted by Aberdeen; later he modified his subject of study to

Trevor-Roper, Master of Peterhouse and recently
ennobled as Lord Dacre, in the early 1980s.

'The Anglican Church in Nyasaland and Malawi, 1861–1975'*
and was given permission to spend several months studying in
Africa.

Trevor-Roper discovered this retrospectively, in 1980, when
Peters applied for a British Academy grant to fund his further
studies. Peters must have been informed that such grants were
not made to students writing theses for higher degrees, but he
was now talking of writing a book rather than continuing to a
Ph.D. By this time Trevor-Roper had retired as Regius Professor; indeed he was no longer in Oxford, having accepted an
invitation to become Master of Peterhouse, one of the oldest

---

* The former British protectorate of Nyasaland became known as Malawi on
gaining independence in 1964.

and most conservative of the Cambridge colleges. Nor was he any longer Trevor-Roper, for the professor had become a lord. In 1979, in one of her first acts as prime minister, Mrs Thatcher had raised him to the peerage and he had chosen the title Lord Dacre of Glanton. In his valedictory speech as Regius Professor, the newly ennobled Lord Dacre recalled the words of Evelyn Waugh during one of their public spats in the *New Statesman* twenty-six years earlier. 'One honourable course is open to Mr Trevor-Roper,' Waugh had written. 'He should change his name and seek a livelihood at Cambridge.' The retiring Regius Professor expressed regret that Waugh was no longer alive to savour this little victory.

In contemplating Peters's grant application, Trevor-Roper asked himself how Peters had financed his two trips to Malawi. Peters stated that his costs had been 'met from personal resources' but Trevor-Roper doubted this, and it seems that Peters had actually been funded by an Anglican mission agency, the United Society for the Propagation of the Gospel (USPG), where one or two staff members were reported to have 'swallowed him whole'.

Two referees supported Peters's application for a grant from the British Academy: his supervisor, the Reverend Dr Adrian Hastings (now somewhat disillusioned) and the Right Reverend Donald Arden, Archbishop of Central Africa and Bishop of Southern Malawi. (The bishop and his wife had been Peters's hosts during his two stays in Malawi; they found him strange, and Mrs Arden was slightly puzzled when he presented her with two pieces of china.) 'I believe this project to be of considerable importance,' the bishop had written in his reference supporting the application to the British Academy. 'The Revd. Robert

Peters seems to me well qualified to undertake this task.' The bishop characterised Peters as 'an extremely hard worker ... He has a quick mind and is able to penetrate to the essentials of a situation.' Like so many others before him, the bishop was initially convinced by Peters, to the extent of advocating that he should be restored to holy orders, 'if not in England, at least in Scotland and Central Africa, with Canterbury's positive assent'. This suggestion was vetoed by Lambeth Palace.

His other referee, Dr Hastings, was much more equivocal, his reservations detectable in his reference. 'His previous work on sixteenth century church history makes one hope that he will be able to look at the Malawian church from a fresh angle,' wrote Hastings, 'although he has come to African history rather late in life.' He admitted that he had not yet seen any written work from his pupil 'and cannot, therefore, comment on it'. The British Academy refused Peters's application for a grant.

Peters had long craved a higher degree, to supplement his MA from Manchester; but by 1981 he no longer needed Aberdeen, as he was now sporting a doctorate from 'Geneva' – not the Swiss city, but a theological college in North Carolina with a reputation for open-handedness in dispensing degrees. Peters wrote to Hastings's head of department, Professor Andrew Walls, announcing his departure. He had been offered, and accepted, he said, a country parish in Donegal, which, though taking up the bulk of his time, would leave sufficient for writing: 'the Bishop is very insistent on that'.

Naturally, I shall miss the academic scene, but, apart from any
other consideration, the present uncertainties and tensions
in the academic world (perhaps the reasons for some of the

curious and inexplicable appointments these days) leave me in no doubt about what I ought to do. The tradition of the scholar-parson is honourable and well established, especially in the Church of Ireland, and if I can add my mite I shall be more than gratified.

There is no evidence in the file to indicate that Trevor-Roper ever knew of Peters's intent to settle in rural Ireland, which was soon superseded anyway. Perhaps Peters never reached Donegal, for only three months after writing the letter announcing his acceptance of a parish there, he was living in a cottage attached to Dundas Castle in South Queensferry, a few miles west of Edinburgh – as Trevor-Roper would discover by reading a pompous letter from Peters, published in the business pages of *The Times*, complaining about bank charges levied by Barclays. To the increasing number of those in the know about Peters, it was strange how he would risk exposure in print – almost as if he wanted to be caught, or perhaps to confess his sins. One wonders if he ever owned up to them in the confessional.

Trevor-Roper had received a cutting of the letter from Alan Bell, Assistant Keeper at the National Library of Scotland. There had been an exchange of correspondence between the two men some months before, after Bell had alerted Trevor-Roper to the news that Peters was a candidate for membership of the Society of Antiquaries of Scotland. In response, Trevor-Roper sent Bell his 'résumé' of Peters's career. 'Scotland is the only part of these islands in which he is (apparently) unblown,' he wrote in his covering letter:

I do not wish to blow him there. I am happy to think that he has found a cosy nest, if only a gull's nest, on that remote and apparently innocent coast. There let him nestle, so long as the hospitable gulls will accommodate him and feed him with sea snails and sprats from their teeming waters. But he should not be allowed into reputable scholarly societies: he will only use the title for further fraud.

'What a remarkable document you have sent me,' replied Bell. 'The man's staying-power is wonderful.' He was able to add a snippet of his own to Trevor-Roper's history:

In the 1950s he was well known at the Institute of Historical Research, where the automatic doors of the Senate House lift used to open to reveal him in a clinch with one of the secretaries – perhaps 'wife' or 'wives' to be ...

Then Peters reappeared in the Manchester area. On 28 May 1982 an announcement appeared in the *Church Times* celebrating the fortieth anniversary of his ordination, with no mention that he had been subsequently defrocked, citing instead two verses from Psalm 118:

The Lord hath chastened me sore: but he hath not given me over unto death.
Open to me the gates of righteousness: I will go into them, and I will praise the Lord.

Was this a coded message to the recently appointed Bishop of Manchester, Stanley Booth-Clibborn? Peters had applied to the bishop for permission to officiate within the diocese. When Gavin White got to hear of this, he wrote to the bishop, who replied that he had heard the sad tale of Peters's 'marriage difficulties', but that the rest was new to him. Booth-Clibborn agreed to consult Lambeth Palace.

One Sunday, before the service at the Anglo-Catholic Church of St Hilda's, Prestwich, the visiting preacher, a canon from Manchester Cathedral, was standing around in the sacristy with the other clergy, who were chatting in small groups, when he was approached by a short, rotund man in robes who introduced himself as 'the Reverend Dr Robert Peters'. He had first appeared there some weeks earlier, and had been accepted and invited to robe for Mass. It was obvious to the canon that Peters had made a beeline for him as the senior man present, and he formed the impression that Peters had 'mugged up on me' beforehand. Peters intimated that he was in Manchester doing some work at the university. The conversation quickly moved on to Oxford, the canon's alma mater, with Peters hinting loftily that he had some position there, perhaps a research fellowship. A few days after this encounter the Bishop of Manchester, presumably acting on instructions from Lambeth Palace, circulated a letter forbidding Peters from any kind of role in ministrations throughout the diocese. This caused some embarrassment at St Hilda's.

Peters was soon on the move again, heading south: in 1982 he was reported to have taken up a position as a senior lecturer in the Uyo College of Education, Nigeria. Nothing is known of his progress there. But later in the year he was once again spied in Oxford. Then, on 1 March 1983, a notice in *The Times* announced that 'The Rev Dr R. P. Peters' had been appointed 'Director of Theological Studies, University College, Buckland'. This institution, founded in 1963 and located in a large Oxfordshire stately

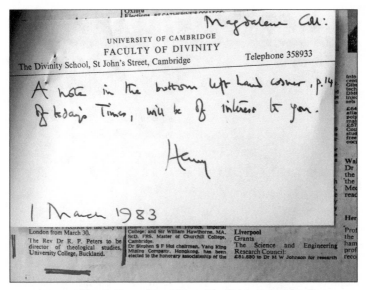

A note to Trevor-Roper from Henry Chadwick, Regius Professor
of Divinity at Cambridge, attaching a clipping from *The Times*.

home, prepared students for examinations accredited by other
universities. It is perhaps not too cynical to suggest that it bene-
fited from its proximity to, and apparent connection with, the
University of Oxford: University College, Oxfordshire, could be
confused by the credulous with University College, Oxford. In a
postcard to Alan Bell, who had recognised Peters outside Black-
well's bookshop carrying a large shopping bag, Trevor-Roper
advised him not to do anything to disturb Peters in his new
home: 'He is bogus, but so is Buckland Univ[ersity] Coll[ege]:
they are fit for each other.'

One evening in March 1983 the Master of Peterhouse turned
on the television, intending to watch the news, and was startled

MASTERMIND CON BY HOAX PARSON

By ANDREW DRUMMOND

MILLIONS of TV viewers watching Mastermind last Sunday were tricked by one of the contestants who posed as a respectable clergyman.

What nobody knew was that the Rev Robert Peters was an unfrocked parson—kicked out of the Church after a bigamy scandal. Unsuspecting quiz presenter Magnus Magnusson introduced Peters as "a minister of religion" from Didcot, Oxfordshire."

In his specialist subject on the life of Dr William Temple, a former Archbishop of Canterbury, Peters got seven questions right and nine wrong.

He went on to score 12 in the general knowledge round and ended up joint third.

SCANDAL

At one point Magnus Magnusson mentioned that 63-year-old Peters was director of theological studies for an Oxford college.

The impostor did not "pass" on any questions. It wasn't quite like that later when I confronted him at University College, Buckland, Oxford.

He told me he had a degree from Manchester University. Then I asked him: "Are you the same Rev Peters, alias Parkins, who was unfrocked in 1953 by the Church of England after a bigamy scandal?"

He replied: "Go away."

MAGNUS: Hoodwinked

I said: "Which church do you belong to?"

He said: "I'm not saying."

As I asked: "Do you have a record of . . ," he interrupted with: "Leave these premises or I'll call the police."

I said: "I've started so I'll finish. Do you have a record of lying to obtain teaching jobs?"

He replied: "Your ques-

tions are impudent. I've never heard of Mr Parkins."

But I can reveal that Peters of Maddon Farm, Didcot, IS the Mr Peters who clashed in 1953 . . . "After 32 years of dishonesty and two bigamous marriages the days of folly are over."

Parkins became a Church of England priest in 1942. He married Miss Brunton, then wed Margaret Gloddaig bigamously.

In 1956, now calling himself Peters he had himself into a research job at Magdalen College, Oxford.

Three years later came his second bigamous marriage to New Zealander Marie Baillie.

In 1973 he was charging students £130 a time for worthless certificates in theology.

One of Peters's current bosses, Mr John Kitely, a director of the Buckland College said: "The college was and is satisfied as to the legitimacy of his academic qualifications."

'I've started, so I'll finish. Do you have a record of lying to obtain teaching jobs?' Cutting from the *News of the World*, 3 April 1983.

to see a familiar figure on the screen, appearing as a contestant on BBC's *Mastermind* programme, dressed in a dog collar and introduced as 'Dr Robert Peters, Minister of Religion'. He was described to the unsuspecting television audience as Director of Religious Studies at a college of Lancaster University, an institution with which in reality he had no connection. (The 'college' turned out to be a hall of residence.) Peters's chosen subject was the life of William Temple, former Archbishop of Canterbury; he answered seven questions right and nine wrong. He did better in the general knowledge round, scoring twelve points, ending the contest in joint third place (out of four).

The following Sunday, a piece appeared in the *News of the World*, under the heading 'MASTERMIND CON BY HOAX PARSON', sandwiched between a provocative photograph of 'model' Linda Lusardi and a story about how Bob Geldof and Paula Yates had become 'proud parents' of their first child. 'Millions of TV viewers watching *Mastermind* last Sunday were tricked by one of the contestants who posed as a respectable clergyman,' revealed the *News of the World*. The story provided some juicy details from Peters's past. 'The impostor did not "pass" on any questions,' the reporter informed his readers; 'it wasn't quite like that later when I confronted him at University College, Buckland, Oxford.' Having accosted Peters, he asked, 'Are you the same Rev. Peters, alias Parkins, who was unfrocked in 1953 [sic] by the Church of England after a bigamy scandal?' Peters ordered him to go away. The reporter persisted: 'Which church do you belong to?' Peters refused to answer this question, so the reporter tried another: 'Do you have a record of –' He was interrupted in mid-flow by Peters, providing him with the opportunity to make use of Magnus Magnusson's catchphrase: 'I've started, so I'll finish. Do you have a record of lying to obtain teaching jobs?' By now flustered, Peters blurted out, 'Your questions are impudent, I've never heard of Mr Parkins,' before turning on his heel and walking swiftly away. Questioned afterwards about Peters, a director of Buckland was quoted as saying that the college was 'satisfied as to the legitimacy of his academic qualifications'.

At Peterhouse Trevor-Roper was having some trouble of his

own. Neither of his two elderly predecessors had succeeded in mastering the college fellowship. In such a small community – a mere two dozen Fellows in 1980 – an organised clique could exert a controlling influence. As elsewhere, the bachelor dons spent more time in college, especially in the evenings, when they dined together in hall. This made it easier for them to coordinate their actions. For the decade before Trevor-Roper's arrival as Master, a small coterie of around half a dozen such dons in effect ran the business of the governing body, while the rest looked on or away. Some of the other Fellows referred to them as 'vampires', because they emerged after dark; Trevor-Roper (now, of course, Lord Dacre) generally referred to them as the 'mafia'. Most were in early middle age when he took office as Master. They were not all of one mind: they included Catholics, Anglicans and atheists; historians and mathematicians; homosexuals and heterosexuals. One Fellow described them as being like overlapping spotlights focused on a single point. What united them, Trevor-Roper decided, was a hatred of liberalism. They had ensured that Peterhouse was one of the last colleges in Cambridge to resist moves to admit women. In voting for his election as Master, they had assumed that Trevor-Roper was as reactionary as they were. But though conservative in his politics, Trevor-Roper was liberal in his thinking, and much more combative than his predecessors. Soon after arriving at the college he had clashed with the ruling clique, and gradually the clashes had escalated into open conflict, so obvious that it began to be reported in the newspapers. Shortly after the first clash one old Peterhouse hand was overheard speaking contemptuously about the mafia. 'They are such fools,' he declared. 'They thought that they were electing a Tory, and never realised that they were electing a Whig.'

The best-known Master of recent times had been another historian, Herbert Butterfield, head of the college from 1955 until 1968, whose thinking had helped to shape the attitudes of his Peterhouse disciples. Butterfield had been a Tory of a very different stamp from Trevor-Roper: Methodist, pro-appeasement, illiberal. In his book *Our Age*, Noel Annan would describe him as 'a radical conservative'. Trevor-Roper was amused to discover from Geoffrey Lampe that his predecessor had been kind to Peters and had taken him seriously. But the satisfaction that the new Master took in Butterfield's embarrassment would be as nothing to the glee his enemies felt when Trevor-Roper himself suffered a mortifying humiliation. Only a few weeks after the parson was exposed in the *News of the World*, the former professor would himself be publicly pilloried, after making a catastrophic mistake: he authenticated a cache of diaries as those of Adolf Hitler.

Hitler's name remained potent. Almost forty years after his death, there was enormous interest in his life and thoughts. Historians continued to debate vigorously his motives and intentions. The appetite for books, newspaper and magazine articles, radio and television programmes and feature films about Hitler remained insatiable. So the 'discovery' of his diaries, announced at a press conference in Germany and purchased at great expense by a combine of media conglomerates, attracted intense public interest, making headlines across the globe. Even at the press conference, however, their authenticity was questioned. Trevor-Roper, appearing as the 'expert' who had lent his authority to the discovery, began to backtrack. He seemed both impulsive and indecisive, an easy target for ridicule. In the academic arena Trevor-Roper remained deft and deadly, but in the glare of publicity he stumbled like a wounded animal. His old foe A. L.

Rowse was unable to resist the opportunity to insert the knife into his former Oxford colleague (whom he had once considered his protégé) in the *Daily Mail*. His article, headed 'The Trial of Lord Dacre', described the Master of Peterhouse (then aged sixty-nine) as 'a young man in a hurry'.

A crowd of camera crews and reporters set up camp in Trumpington Street outside the Master's Lodge, leaning against the doorbell and shouting questions through the letter box. Trevor-Roper stayed out of sight, his policy to say nothing until the position clarified. 'For days after my return [from Germany], my life was torture,' he noted in his diary. He was besieged, cut off from the college by the waiting pressmen. On one occasion, he shinned over the garden wall into the car park next to the lodge and begged a lift from one of the Fellows who was about to leave. While the Master of Peterhouse crouched on the floor, the Nobel Prize-winning scientist drove out past the besiegers, dropping his furtive passenger near the entrance to the deer park, the back way into the college.

Within two weeks of the press conference, the diaries had been proved to be forgeries. It was arguably the greatest hoax of modern times and certainly the most widely publicised. The forger was revealed to be a low-life con man called Konrad Kujau. The German journalist who had purchased the diaries from Kujau refused to believe that such a man could have been responsible for their manufacture: 'he's far too primitive.' But Kujau's guilt was soon beyond dispute. A flamboyant character, he cheerfully accepted a prison sentence, perhaps realising that he had enjoyed a good run.

It was ironic that Trevor-Roper, of all people, should have been fooled by such a crude forgery. One might suppose that, through his studies of Backhouse and Peters, he would be the last person to be so duped. It is hard to understand how one so critical could be so careless. But Trevor-Roper was not the first, and no doubt would not be the last, scholar to be the victim of fraud. Moreover, he had been lied to: he was told that the paper and the ink used in the diaries had been tested (it had not); that the handwriting had been compared with a sample of Hitler's and shown to be the same (it had, but the sample of Hitler's hand originated from the same forger); and that the provenance of the diaries was known (the story of their discovery was soon shown to be false).

Trevor-Roper expected the others responsible for the fiasco of the Hitler diaries to take their share of the blame. In this he was disappointed. He was not the only one to succumb to the fraud, but he was the one to whom most of the odium attached. The damage to his reputation was permanent and irreparable.

There has been much speculation about the reasons for his mistake. It has often been said that his German was not adequate to the job, but this is untrue. He was not fluent in German, but he could speak it well enough to hold a conversation. He read German books and documents, and often received letters written in German, though he usually chose to reply in English. His German was certainly adequate to the rudimentary task of reading diary entries. The problem he encountered in this case was twofold: first, that the handwriting was so spidery as to be largely illegible, and second, that the diaries were written in an antiquated script, which most Germans themselves cannot read.

Trevor-Roper's mistake was to have allowed himself to be hustled into giving an opinion before he was ready; to have given an opinion based on the outward appearance of the diaries rather than their content; and to have relied on what he was told about them, rather than what he had ascertained personally.

The charge of hubris has been made against him. It was certainly true that he was arrogant. His brilliance made him impatient with the ponderous progress typical of historical study. He often cut corners. So much work had come his way as a result of the worldwide success of *The Last Days of Hitler* that he had perhaps grown careless about it. 'Trevor-Roper thought that he had taken out a patent on Hitler,' complained A. J. P. Taylor in the 1960s. Yet far from being overconfident, there was a sense in which he had begun to feel marginalised. Perhaps he hoped that his involvement with the Hitler diaries would restore him to the central position he had once occupied in Hitler studies. Of course, it had the opposite effect.

By 1983 the President of Magdalen was Keith Griffin, an American economist. In December of that year he received a letter marked 'confidential' from 'The Reverend Dr R. P. Peters', sent from an address in Marston, on the outskirts of Oxford. Peters requested an interview during the vacation. 'The matter on which I should like your advice is (for me, at any rate) a delicate one,' he wrote, 'because nearly thirty years ago I behaved badly towards the college, where I was doing research, and if it were possible for the record to be "squared" and the ambition of a lifetime realised now at the age of 65* – I should be more than happy.' Peters referred modestly to the letters after his name: 'As you will see, I have achieved some academic standing from Manchester University and Geneva Theological College – also

---

* For once Peters was not lying about his age.

A handwritten letter from 'The Reverend Dr R. P. Peters' to the President of Magdalen, 9 December 1983. The annotation below the date in another hand reads 'Matric [ulated] MT [Michaelmas term] '57'.

Gray's Inn, of which I am privileged to be a Prizeman* – but every time I pass Magdalen I <u>long</u> for the "years that the locust has eaten"† to be restored, as it were.' He felt that the first step would be a 'very frank discussion' with the President.

Griffin's reply was brief:

> As you can well imagine, there is a thick file on you in our archives, and I have just spent an hour or so sifting through it. Having done so, I believe little purpose would be served in a meeting. Old wounds would inevitably be re-opened to no effect. I suggest that you and the college both try to forget the past.

---

* A non-existent qualification. Peters was never a member of Gray's Inn, though a man of approximately the same age called David Robert Peters was admitted there in 1948. This was during the period when Peters was abroad, having fled the country to avoid a trial for bigamy. It seems possible that at some point Peters became aware that he had a near namesake who was a member of Gray's Inn and decided to turn this to his advantage by borrowing his identity.

† 'And I will restore to you the years that the locust hath eaten, the cankerworm, and the caterpillar, and the palmerworm, my great army which I sent among you.' Joel 2:25.

PART III

1983–2005

NINE

The apartheid parson

Trevor-Roper's log of the parson's progress ceases in 1983. There is only one further item in his dossier, a letter from a librarian written several years later. For the remaining twenty years of his life, until his death in January 2003, the professor showed no further interest in Robert Peters. Though he had pursued Peters for almost a quarter of century, he would never confront his quarry. Their only face-to-face meeting had been in Trevor-Roper's office in the Oxford history faculty in the winter of 1958, when the parson had come to see him with his strange tale of clerical persecution. After that initial encounter there had never been any direct communication between them. Trevor-Roper had spotted Peters in 1965, addressing a congress in Vienna, but Peters had recognised him and made himself scarce afterwards. Whether Peters was aware that Trevor-Roper was following his progress so closely remains unknown. One suspects that he must have learned, from Rupp if from nobody else, that the professor was on his tail.

Why did Trevor-Roper give up the chase? Until this point he had always enjoyed Peters's exploits, taking delight in the fact that so many grandees had been taken in by the bogus parson.

But after the searing experience of the Hitler diaries, after enduring so much humiliation, he seems to have felt otherwise. Perhaps he no longer found charlatanry quite so amusing. In the aftermath of this personal disaster, others may have thought it tactless to send him further material about such a persistent confidence trickster as Peters. And Trevor-Roper himself may have reflected that he was no longer in a position to publish anything on Peters; to do so would only be to invite further ridicule.

In any case, Peters himself had once again disappeared over the horizon. Back in 1967, after Peters had been deported from America for a third and final time, Professor Brundage had speculated in a letter to Trevor-Roper about where he might try next. One possibility, he suggested, was the Antipodes:

> It has been some time since Peters made an attempt to place himself in one of their universities. Another possibility would be South Africa; possibly he found the Calvinistic climate at Hope College sufficiently warming that he might want to strike out on a new track.

This was a good guess. South Africa was indeed where Peters headed next, albeit fifteen years on, to take up a post as Rector of the Anglican church of Virginia, in the Orange Free State. Before his arrival, there had been heated arguments at meetings of the local Diocesan Standing Committee about the wisdom of appointing a man unknown to almost everyone, but the Bishop of Bloemfontein, the Right Reverend Tom Stanage, had steamrollered the appointment. He assured the other members of the committee that Peters was an excellent choice, and that he would provide all the necessary documentation when he arrived from

England. This of course never materialised. In fact the doubters would be proved right and Bishop Tom was soon disillusioned with his find, whom he would eventually come to think of as 'the most wicked man I have ever met'. After only a few months Peters would be asked to leave, for causing 'pastoral havoc'. It would be interesting to know what Peters had done to upset people so much, but the details remain disappointingly elusive. When he heard that Peters had surfaced in South Africa, Gavin White sent a full report on him to interested parties, but too late to prevent his appointment. 'I cannot understand why these bishops are so easily fooled,' he would comment afterwards.

With his departure for South Africa, Peters recedes into the distance. The closure of Trevor-Roper's dossier means that nobody was keeping track of his progress. The trail had gone cold by the time I came to pick it up, more than thirty years later. No written records of his five years in South Africa have come to light. Half a lifetime later, some of the people he encountered have died, while the memories of those who remain have faded. It also seems likely that some in South Africa, as elsewhere, are too embarrassed to recall how they were so completely taken in. Peters had always been adept at keeping a low profile and at moving on to fresh pastures before the results of his misdeeds caught up with him. In the confusion of South Africa in what we now know to have been the last years of apartheid, it was easy to hide. All that remains for us is a series of glimpses, as the recognisable figure appears briefly in silhouette, before ducking below the horizon.

Despite increasing pressure for reform, a system of apartheid ('separate development') still prevailed in South Africa in the mid-1980s, when Peters arrived there. Since 1948 racial segregation had been imposed in almost every aspect of life, from housing to park benches. Though many Christians opposed apartheid and the Anglican church was one of the few institutions in which whites and blacks could mix on equal terms, it remained true that white clergy in the Orange Free State would have served exclusively white parishes, while black clergy covered much the same area, serving very much larger Sesotho-speaking congregations. There would have been very little contact between the two. It is difficult to imagine Peters in a small town in the Orange Free State, even as rector of a small minority Anglican and English-speaking parish. Afrikaans would have been the lingua franca, and the English-speaking minority would have adopted much of the Afrikaner way of life. Peters was not the type of man to recline out of doors on a deckchair, eating barbecued meat and corn on the cob with his fingers.

As time went by, rumours spread that Peters was a man with a past, though these remained unsubstantiated, and Peters himself never opened up about his life before coming to South Africa. Locals had the impression that he regarded them with disdain, feeling that they were not up to his high intellectual standards; even at social gatherings, with wives present, he would discuss only church business, or perhaps some recondite topic such as New Testament Greek. Colleagues observed that Peters treated his wife like a doormat. He always dressed in a black suit with a clerical collar, making no concession to the South African climate. He seemed to cultivate an aura of mystery and was wont to appear at intervals without warning. On one occasion he took an archdeacon of the diocese aside and showed him what he said was a very valuable old prayer book. He would never let it out of his sight so long as he lived, he said, and told the archdeacon that after his death his wife would ensure that it was preserved for future generations. On another occasion he presented the archdeacon's bewildered wife with a set of 24-carat gold-plated teaspoons.

After being asked to leave three parishes in little over two years, Peters applied for a school chaplaincy at St Mary's College, Bloemfontein. (School chaplaincies were often the refuge of would-be academics and those who had failed in the parochial ministry.) Though successful in obtaining the post, he was soon sacked, after being accused of fraud and dishonesty.

Then he took up a post as a lecturer – or possibly, if one believes his claims, senior lecturer – at the Federal Theological Seminary (Fedsem) in Edendale, Natal. This was an ecumenical college, drawing together the Anglican, Methodist and Presbyterian Churches, founded in the early 1960s to provide theological education for candidates deprived entry to whites-only religious institutions. It was in some ways ironic that Peters should be recruited to teach at such an institution, because he made little effort to conceal his disdain for 'non-whites'. A colleague at Fedsem, a Scot who, like Peters, had studied at Aberdeen, felt that Peters was an unpleasant man with no regard for anyone, of whatever skin colour: self-possessed, arrogant and opinionated. When he suggested that Peters should speak more slowly during lectures to help students take in what he was saying, Peters retorted that students could not understand him, because of his Scottish accent. Gradually colleagues realised that Peters was a 'stirrer', a man who made a habit of telling one member of staff that another had criticised his work, withdrawing before the inevitable eruption occurred. Once it became obvious that he was intent on making trouble, he was summoned to a meeting of the academic board to be disciplined, but he packed and left the seminary during the night before the meeting. The official explanation for his departure was that he had been dismissed for incompetence and incitement of racial and ecumenical tensions. To be dismissed for inciting racial tensions in apartheid-era South Africa, even from a relatively liberal institution such as Fedsem, was a striking achievement.

Before he left, Peters had preached what turned out to be a valedictory sermon, taking as his subject the American term for graduation, 'commencement'. He saw this as a new beginning, with all its concomitant opportunities, rather than as the ending of a period of preparation for ministry. He delivered his sermon dressed in elaborate vestments, which did little for his squat frame; one member of the congregation likened him to a Buddha with clothes on.

After quitting the Federal Theological Seminary, Peters took up a post as Rector of Vryheid, one of the largest towns in the region bordering the Indian Ocean now known as KwaZulu-Natal. Under the apartheid system, some of the rural areas and townships where the black population of KwaZulu-Natal was concentrated formed a nominally self-governing 'Bantustan', but Vryheid and the other important towns remained set aside for whites. Within a short period Peters had so upset his parishioners that they appealed to the Bishop of Zululand to intervene. When Peters refused to resign, arguing that the bishop had no authority over him, he had to be forcibly removed, in a confrontation that took place at the very door of the church in Vryheid. The reasons given by the bishop for his dismissal were pastoral incompetence and defiance of canonical authority.

Then Peters took up a post as a lecturer at a college in the small town of Hebron, north-west of Pretoria, in Bophuthatswana, another of the semi-autonomous homelands set aside for blacks under the apartheid system. Bophuthatswana was the most dispersed of the Bantustans, with scattered black townships adjacent to white towns in parts of what are now Northern Cape, North West, Gauteng and Free State provinces. It was politically volatile: there was an attempted coup in Bophuthatswana in February 1988, put down by the South African army, and there was to be another in 1990. Any manifestation of dissent was ruthlessly suppressed. The college was one of thirteen teacher training colleges attached to the University of Bophuthatswana in Mafeking (now part of the University of the North West).

Peters proclaimed himself an Oxford graduate, with a Ph.D. in church history, and the author of several important books. He continued to wear a dog collar at all times, and boasted of officiating and preaching in the cathedral at Bloemfontein. Another theologian who met him several times during this period describes him as 'somewhat arrogant'. He was said to have been a tolerably good, if somewhat boring, lecturer. But in any case he did not stay long, being dismissed when his 'qualifications' were found to be false.

Once more, Peters ducked out of sight. His subsequent movements remain obscure. All that is known is that he was deported, probably in the summer of 1988. This was becoming a habit with Peters: he had been deported from Switzerland, probably from Australia, from the United States (three times), from Canada (twice) and now from South Africa. After his forcible return to England, he would claim that he had been expelled from South Africa as a campaigner against apartheid. This seems improbable. There is a rumour that he was deported because he had been convicted of stealing a car, which is plausible, given that he had been prosecuted in the past for failing to make the repayments after obtaining a car on credit. But the most likely reason is more prosaic: that he was deported simply because his visa would not allow him, as an unemployed alien, to remain.

TEN

In which the parson appoints himself principal (reprise)

By the autumn of 1988 Peters was back in Cambridge, looking for work. Bishop Ronald Gordon, the Archbishop of Canterbury's chief of staff, warned a potential employer against engaging him.

By the time Peters arrived in Cambridge, Trevor-Roper had just left, his seven-year term as Master of Peterhouse having elapsed. His successor would be Henry Chadwick, who until 1979 had been Dean of Christ Church and since then had been Regius Professor of Divinity at Cambridge, in succession to Geoffrey Lampe. By becoming Master of Peterhouse, Chadwick was the first person in more than four centuries to have been a head of house in both the ancient universities. Chadwick was in a hurry to move into the Master's Lodge so that his daughter could be married from there, and put pressure on his predecessor to leave. As he left Peterhouse, rather more hurriedly than he might have wished, Trevor-Roper looked back on 'seven wasted years'.

His new house was in Didcot, not far from Oxford, where

coincidentally Peters had been living five years earlier, in his short spell as Director of Theological Studies at University College, Buckland. The Old Rectory was a dignified house, with high ceilings and well-proportioned rooms. But it was surrounded by an unlovely modern estate, in a town dominated by a huge power station, with little character and few amenities, and no access by foot to open country. Trevor-Roper would refer mockingly to Didcot as 'the Thebes of the Thames Valley'.

When Peters applied for a reader's ticket at the Cambridge University Library, he was recognised as a 'very old friend' by the Librarian, F. W. Ratcliffe, who informed Trevor-Roper of the fact by letter, the last item in the professor's dossier, several years after the previous one. Ratcliffe had come across Peters before, in the early 1960s, in his role as University Librarian at Manchester, and after all this time knew quite a lot about him – 'he has been in and out of my professional life for over thirty years'. At Ratcliffe's suggestion, his deputy wrote to Peters, seeking clarification of his status as a clergyman; Peters's reply was 'a masterpiece of righteous indignation'. He appealed to the chairman of the Syndicate, the library's governing body, and his application was referred to the next meeting of the Syndics. 'I am looking forward to that,' wrote Ratcliffe.

History does not record whether Peters's application to the university library was ultimately successful, or whether he was once again thwarted. Ratcliffe, who retired in 1994, does not remember what happened, though it is hard to imagine that Peters's bluff would not have been called. Be that as it may, over the next few years Peters was often to be seen – invariably dressed in black and wearing a dog collar – 'beavering away' at Tyndale House in Cambridge, one of the world's largest libraries of biblical studies. Other scholars who encountered him there found him friendly, if somewhat mysterious: a small, squat man, almost hunchbacked, with sharp, watchful eyes. He styled himself 'Dr Peters' and would throw out hints about past achievements, implying that he was too modest to go into details.

There is evidence of his reading in his review, published in *History Today*, of three books, in which he praised especially a volume by A. G. Dickens, former professor of history at King's College, London, and Director of the Institute of Historical Research. (Dickens was often cited alongside Rupp as a referee in Peters's job applications.) 'It is good to have this valuable collection of essays by the "Master" of English Reformation studies,' Peters wrote grandly. 'To read them again is to breathe the refined air of mature scholarship.' He singled out one essay in particular, for providing 'further insights into the ecclesiological and social concerns of the Yorkshire priest Robert Parkyn, curate of Adwick-le-Street, a stolid ecclesiastical conservative ...' Was this a private joke? If so, it was his first on record. One does not associate Peters with humour.

Martyn Percy* was one of the young scholars who came across Peters at Tyndale House. He was impressed when Peters let it be known that he was a contributor to the *Oxford Dictionary of the Christian Church*.† As an ordained minister himself, he

---

* In 2014 Percy would become Dean of Christ Church, the post held by Cuthbert Simpson and Henry Chadwick, among others.

† The name 'R. Peters, Oxford' is listed among the 250-odd contributors to the second edition of the *Oxford Dictionary of the Christian Church*, edited by F. L. Cross and E. A. Livingstone and published in 1974. The entries are

had been interested when Peters implied that he was assisting in services in a local parish. But he was warned by other readers at the library to 'be careful' about Peters; 'he's not what he seems to be.' Over coffee one day at Tyndale House, Percy ventured a question: 'Do you mind my asking why you aren't in *Crockford*?'

'Ah well,' replied Peters, not at all flustered, 'you see, a number of us who were in South Africa were offered the opportunity to be in *Crockford*, but I refused.' This was a rather feeble piece of obfuscation, but Percy let it pass.

Anyone who knew Peters soon became aware of his vehement opposition to women's ordination, then a much-debated and contentious issue within the Anglican Communion. Peters quickly became abusive when the subject came up for discussion. In 1992, when the General Synod voted in favour of women's ordination, Peters described it as 'a dark day for the Church'. He told Percy that he would be writing to the Bishop of Ely to 'resign his Anglican orders', and that he intended to be received into the Catholic Church, and in due course to be ordained as a Catholic priest. Percy expressed surprise that they might contemplate receiving a married pensioner into their priestly ranks, but Peters was too angry at the result of the vote to listen to reason. Percy remembers leaving Tyndale House that day and looking back to see Peters standing at an upstairs window, his thumb turned down in a gesture of disapproval. After the first woman was ordained, in 1994, he kept a file entitled 'Women priests', with quotation marks around the word 'priests'. He would refer to dog collars worn by women as 'bitch collars'.

---

unattributed. It has been suggested to me that the entry for 'archdeacon', which cites Peters's own work on the archdeaconry of St Albans, may be his.

Percy persisted. When, at a subsequent encounter, he asked Peters why he did not appear to hold a licence from the diocese of Ely, Peters erupted in fury, accusing him of 'casting aspersions'. Percy was reminded of Rumpelstiltskin, stamping his foot in rage. He noticed that Peters gave him a wide berth after that.

Tyndale House was a haunt of young scholars studying for higher degrees. Most were eager to gain some experience of teaching and to earn money by taking on paid work, even of the most menial kind. The experience of one of these, Philip Johnston, was typical of several, even though, being in his mid-thirties, he was older than many. He was already teaching part-time at a local evangelical college, but when Peters offered him more work he was inclined to accept. Peters explained that he had recently set up the Cambridge Religious Studies Centre, a small, non-denominational theological college, and was looking for help. He had started, he said, in a fledgling way, offering distance-learning courses leading to the University of London Bachelor of Divinity (BD) and the Cambridge Diploma in Religious Studies, with face-to-face teaching confined to three Saturdays each term. In general the students were middle-aged, many of them schoolteachers. Often the tutors were younger than the students.

Johnston took up Peters's invitation to visit the Centre, a farmhouse Peters had rented about ten miles west of Cambridge, then on the edge of a village, now part of the new town of Cambourne. An upstairs room had been converted into a chapel, and some other rooms set up as classrooms. One was labelled 'Senior Common Room' – rather pretentiously, Johnston thought. The set-up had a High Church 'feel', which contrasted with his own Low Church background in Northern Ireland. Nevertheless he saw nothing to deter him from accepting the offer.

After Johnston had been working there for a while, Peters promoted him to the post of 'Dean of Studies', and tried to get him to recruit other, younger tutors. He appointed Bryan Spinks, chaplain of Cambridge college, Churchill, as 'Senior Tutor'. Peters himself was 'Principal and Chairman of Trustees'. The 'Bursar', 'Registrar', and 'College Secretary' was Ann Brinded – Mrs Peters, using her maiden name, though her day job was teaching at a local school. (Some of the students did not realise that they were married.) Notionally there was a board of trustees, a miscellaneous collection, many of whom stayed only a few months. Some of these were former students whom Peters had invited to become trustees; none had any experience of academic life at the higher level. But their lack of qualifications was barely relevant, because, like 'the faculty', they rarely met; in practice the running of the Centre was tightly controlled by Peters and his wife.

To Johnston, the profusion of titles in such a small college seemed absurdly grandiose. Tutors were required to wear gowns, in a rule reminiscent of Oxford or Cambridge in the past. (Trevor-Roper had been one of the last Oxford lecturers to insist on students wearing gowns.) Indeed, the Cambridge Religious Studies Centre was a Lilliputian version of Magdalen in the 1950s. Driven out of paradise, Peters had created his own heaven in miniature. On the first teaching day of the academic year, Peters convened an 'assembly' in the living room of the farmhouse: the dozen or so students present were required to stand while the staff processed in, all wearing academic gowns, as if entering to dine at high table in an Oxbridge college. Last of all came the Principal, solemn and ceremonial.

The Cambridge Religious Studies Centre was only a

shoestring operation, with never more than a handful of students. It was registered as a charity. Peters himself was the sole full-time employee, with others paid by the hour. In 1995 the Centre's turnover was estimated at under £25,000, once the costs of validation (payments to the academic body which validated the courses taught there) had been deducted. This was deemed sufficient to cover the costs of teaching and overheads. Manifestly Peters was not in it for the money; but being principal of a college gave him prestige, which he valued much more.

It may seem odd that Peters was able to start up another theological college only a dozen years or so after the collapse of St Aidan's, with the accompanying unwelcome publicity. But few, if any, made the connection. Professor Geoffrey Lampe was no longer around to act as his scourge, having died in 1980; Gordon Rupp had followed him to the grave in 1986. And Trevor-Roper had retired wounded from the struggle. Peters had survived them all. He was not easily deterred: he resembled one of those serial bankrupts who quickly rises again after each collapse. The times were propitious for such a new venture: the 1990s was a decade of schism within the Anglican Communion, when Christians discomforted by the ordination of women and other reforms founded dozens of breakaway churches, some attracting no more than a handful of devotees. Theological colleges proliferated, particularly those offering traditional teaching. In the 1990s one could sit papers for the London BD or the Cambridge Certificate for Theological Studies anywhere, and it was up to the candidate where he or she obtained his or her tuition.

This was a period, too, when small institutions such as the Cambridge Religious Studies Centre began to seek validation from universities for their own syllabuses, often out of a desire to award master's degrees. Peters had approached the University of Hull to request accreditation of a new BA course in religious studies that he wanted to introduce. After examining the proposal and investigating the Centre, Hull's Department of Theology decided to recommend approval. Some concern was expressed that junior staff did the bulk of the teaching, but the investigators found them very competent and the design of the course looked acceptable.

Justin Meggitt, his girlfriend, Melanie Wright, and Jane McLarty were three of the young postgraduates who responded to an advertisement in the *Cambridge Evening News* for suitably qualified people to teach at the Cambridge Religious Studies Centre. Meggitt was disconcerted when Peters referred to one of the former women tutors (perhaps because she had rejected his advances) as 'no better than a prostitute'. Peters seemed to Meggitt to take a prurient interest in sex. Though by this time in his mid-seventies, he was still propositioning young women who came his way. Jane McLarty experienced this on one occasion, when she went to talk to Peters about the courses they were running. At some point during the conversation, when the subject had wandered on to relationships, Peters had put his hand on hers and said something about how one could love a range of people. She rapidly removed her hand from beneath his, stating firmly that she believed in faithfulness within marriage. Another female tutor who had a similar experience was able to turn the tables on him, by threatening to go to the police unless he wrote her a reference.

Peters was not an understanding employer. When Melanie Wright asked for compassionate leave because her mother had died, Peters was signally unsympathetic. 'I don't know why she's making such a big of deal of it,' he said. 'I was back at work the day after my mother died.' Later, when Wright herself became ill, he made shockingly disparaging comments about her to other members of staff. Students, too, were startled by the way he denigrated former tutors: 'I'm afraid that Miss –– has badly let us down this term.' He seemed to think that anyone who left the Centre, for whatever reason, was guilty of betrayal.

Another young scholar recruited by Peters was Nicholas Taylor, who, having recently been awarded his Ph.D., was hoping for an academic career and in the meantime was earning a very modest income as a copy editor and proofreader. In 1993, after presenting a paper at a conference in St Andrews, he was accosted by Peters, dressed as usual in black with dog collar, who identified himself as the Principal of the Cambridge Religious Studies Centre and offered him a part-time post as New Testament tutor. Taylor found this sudden offer from a stranger a little odd, though he was somewhat reassured to hear of Bryan Spinks's involvement, as he knew Spinks to be a respected scholar. Peters described himself as an Anglican priest and said that he had worked in South Africa – though he looked startled when Taylor responded that he had grown up there, and that his own father was an Anglican priest. Peters also mentioned having been chaplain to Gresham's School, and seemed further troubled when Taylor told him that several members of his family and their friends had attended Gresham's over the years.

The following week Taylor visited the Centre, now relocated to another former farmhouse in the village of Buckden, between Huntingdon and St Neots. (Peters and his wife were living nearby in a thatched cottage.) Some bedrooms had been furnished as tutorial rooms and another as a chapel. Hanging on a wall (and used on the Centre's writing paper) was a coat of arms of Peters's own design, along with commemorative shields of Gray's Inn, the University of Hull and other worthy bodies, the whole suggesting a reputable pedigree. Like Martyn Percy before him, Taylor had already ascertained that Peters did not appear in *Crockford*; in the Centre's library he found a Southern African Anglican directory, in which the dates of Peters's ordinations had been altered by hand to ten years later and in which he was credited with a list of degrees somewhat different from the list in the Centre's prospectus. Taylor noticed, too, that he was listed as Robert Parkin Peters, which seemed odd, as Peters had mentioned in passing that he had only one initial. Some weeks later Taylor attended the first Saturday teaching session, where he met other staff (including Bryan Spinks) and students for the first time. During the year that Taylor taught at the Centre there were never more than two or three ordinary tutors, at least one of whom had no degree (and Taylor was therefore expected to audit her classes and mark her students' work); one lasted only a single teaching day.

Justin Meggitt soon began to have doubts about Peters. He noticed that, in the preparation of course materials, the Principal appeared to be passing off other people's work as his own. This prompted him to investigate Peters's academic credentials. He discovered that the doctorate of which Peters was so proud came not from a major European university (as Peters was happy for people to believe), but from 'a small theological college in America that seemed to dish them out wholesale'. Meggitt, who was then just finalising his own doctorate, raised his concerns with his supervisor, and with senior colleagues at the Centre, who did not respond in the way that he had hoped. To them, Peters seemed a little eccentric, perhaps, and too inclined to become embroiled in altercations with the junior staff; but not venal. By this time Meggitt was convinced that Peters was a fraud: feeling isolated and exposed, he resigned, as did his girlfriend, Melanie Wright. He wrote to Professor Lester Grabbe, head of the Department of Theology at Hull, to warn him that Peters might have provided false information about himself and his qualifications. Afterwards Meggitt received a 'without prejudice' letter from Peters, threatening legal action for defamation if he continued his 'campaign of slander'. For a young postgraduate, lacking the resources to defend an action, such a letter was intimidating – as was Peters's threat to write to every university in the land, warning potential employers against him. He made similar threats against Melanie Wright.

Jane McLarty had also quit the Centre. In her resignation letter, which she sent with a covering note to Philip Johnston, she complained about Peters's authoritarian management style: in particular, she found his statement 'I demand obedience from my staff' unacceptable. He had upbraided her for adapting and condensing his material in her lectures. She saw nothing wrong in having done so; indeed, it had been at his request. She felt that he was unnecessarily protective of his own work – not that it was his own, of course. She also felt 'intensely unhappy' about his dismissive attitude towards the students, who were (as she reminded him) their paying customers.

Johnston was aware that Peters was lacking in various ways, though not wholly ignorant; he had obviously picked up a considerable knowledge of theological study, even if haphazardly. He struck Johnston as clever in a devious sense, a man who saw himself alone against the world: in his eyes, everything that went wrong was somebody else's fault. There was a needy side to him – but he didn't want anyone too close. Though they never became friends, Peters would telephone Johnston in the evening and it was hard to get him off the 'phone. Calls would often last an hour or more, so long that Johnston's wife came to resent them. Other members of staff had similar experiences: Justin Meggitt, for example, has a vivid memory of standing by a public telephone in a cold corridor in a postgraduate house of Selwyn College, becoming tired and bored as Peters talked on and on, his monologue a strange combination of 'confidences' about other staff, patronising advice and rambling anecdotes.

While on holiday in South Africa, Nicholas Taylor was doing some digging of his own. He had renewed his former academic contacts, one of whom suggested that he ought to 'ask questions about' Peters: his academic and ecclesiastical credentials had been questioned and there were suspicions of bigamy. On his return to Britain, Taylor found Peters in a panic about the allegations of plagiarism from the two tutors who had resigned, and anxious to know with whom he had spoken in South Africa.

Like Meggitt before him, Taylor had become suspicious that Peters was not all he pretended to be. A family friend, then a solicitor in Diss, Norfolk, recalled that there had been a cleric on the staff at Gresham's who had disappeared rather suddenly and had turned out to be a bigamist. He could not immediately recall the name, but it wasn't Peters; when Taylor offered 'Parkin' he instantly recalled the name: 'Parkins'. Taylor contacted his former supervisor in Durham, who ascertained that Peters did not hold a degree from that university, as he was claiming. A cousin who had worked with Professor Andrew Walls, head of department at Aberdeen while Peters was there, was able to obtain some information from him, mainly about Peters's academic record

. and his conduct in parts of Africa; he also mentioned that aliases were used. A former college chaplain, at the time working at Lambeth Palace, found documents indicating that Parkins alias Peters had been defrocked by the Bishop of Bath and Wells, and that subsequently he had claimed Old Catholic orders. Sheridan Gilley, then Reader in Church History in Durham, put Taylor in touch with Gavin White, who had retired to St Andrews. White had long experience of Peters, whom he had first encountered at the University of Toronto back in the late 1940s. Like Trevor-Roper, he had become suspicious of Peters and begun collecting information about him, which he kept in a dossier. White sent Taylor his version of Peters's curriculum vitae, which he referred to as 'The Life and Crimes of Robert Parkin Peters'.

Alarmed by his discoveries, Taylor contacted Professor Grabbe in Hull to express his concerns. Grabbe had already been alerted by Meggitt that Peters might not be all he claimed to be. Now he urged Taylor to remain in post for the duration of the academic year, 'for the benefit of the students', while he and his colleagues conducted an investigation. They were especially concerned that, although Peters had written some pieces on church history that had been published in well-known and reputable journals, his 'doctorate' appeared worthless. Shortly after, Peters announced at the staff meeting that Hull's Registrar had requested copies of the degree certificates of all staff, which he was refusing to supply. 'What a cheek!' was his comment. Taylor noticed that a photograph of Peters in academic dress had disappeared from the wall. He mentioned to Bryan Spinks, fairly circumspectly, that he had heard 'some comments' about Peters in South Africa.

By this time Professor Grabbe and his colleagues were having serious doubts about Peters. On Grabbe's behalf, Sheridan Gilley had written to Gavin White, who provided a lengthy summary of his experience of Peters over the past forty-six years. 'That he is still active at his age is astonishing,' White wrote in conclusion. 'That he is running a religious centre is appalling. That any university should wish to be quit of him is only too understandable.' Meanwhile Hull's Vice-Chancellor, Professor David Dilks, consulted Kathleen Major, now in retirement in Lincoln. She informed him that she had become suspicious of Peters's claimed credentials at an early stage because of the startling gaps in his knowledge.

When Peters came up to Hull for the moderation of exams (a part of the normal accreditation proceedings required by the university), he and his wife were grilled by two of the Vice-Chancellors. During this interview Peters was furious and blustering; afterwards he appeared thoroughly shaken. He told Bryan Spinks that they had questioned his clerical status and had even suggested that he had married bigamously. (He admitted to Spinks that he had been married before, but maintained that the marriage had been annulled.) They had also (so he said) asked similar questions about Spinks, who was indignant; it was true that he had been divorced, but never 'inhibited' – he had remarried, and the Bishop of Ely had taken him under his wing. He was licensed under seal to the diocese, was chairman of the liturgy committee and also appointed by the archbishops to the Liturgical Commission. As he had done with Adrian Hastings, Peters had knowingly touched a sensitive spot and tied Spinks closer with bonds of fellow feeling.

Following this interview, the authorities in Hull decided to withdraw accreditation from the Centre's degree programme. Undismayed, Peters sought and obtained accreditation from De Montfort, a former polytechnic in Leicester converted into a university* only three years before and fast expanding, though as yet it had no theology department and therefore was arguably less able to assess the worth of the Centre's work. De Montfort's 'Quality Assurance' team pronounced themselves satisfied. The Cambridge Religious Studies Centre was renamed Monkfield College, after the Cambridgeshire farmhouse where it had begun. It again relocated, this time to a house on the eastern side of Oxford, outside the ring road, in the same lane (Lewis Close) where C. S. Lewis had lived.

When Philip Johnston announced that he was leaving to take up a post at St Andrews, he received a letter from a firm of Cambridge solicitors acting on behalf of the college, who threatened to sue him for breach of contract. He took little notice of this empty threat. Peters asked Nicholas Taylor for help in recruiting a replacement for Johnston and to fill other posts – while simultaneously informing him that, if he could not commit to the whole of the forthcoming academic year, he would be replaced. Taylor took the opportunity to resign. In 1996 Bryan Spinks left, after being offered a visiting professorship in America. Monkfield relocated once again, to a large, early Victorian house, surrounded on three sides by an unkempt garden, in the village of Leadenham in Lincolnshire. In a message to students about the move, Peters wrote that 'a very great amount of work remains to be done, inside and outside', and singled out for praise one of their number who had been clearing the garden wilderness, while implicitly criticising those who had not rallied round: 'In earlier days, our students (with husbands/wives) readily offered help – without being asked.'

---

*Peters also approached Coventry, another former polytechnic, which had become a university in 1992.

Students were upset and sometimes irritated by these frequent moves, which were of course inconvenient, and they were dismayed by the rapid turnover of staff. One schoolteacher who began a two-year MA course in 1996 had an excellent supervisor for her first year, who then regrettably left; her successor lasted a term; and his successor, a week. For her final term she was supervised by Peters himself, a dubious privilege, since he would not leave her alone. 'Come and sit round this side of the desk with me,' he would say when she arrived for a supervision. He started telephoning her late at night to engage in personal conversations, like a lover, and sent her suggestive letters – inappropriate on a number of levels, not least because she was gay.

Given that most of the students were middle-aged professional people in mid-career, they might have expected to be afforded a certain degree of respect. In fact the opposite was the case: Peters treated them like schoolchildren and his rule was absolute. He made them conform to a succession of petty regulations and led them to believe that they might not be awarded a degree unless they complied. No excuse was accepted for failure to attend one of the Saturday sessions, not even serious illness. He sneered at the B.Ed., the usual qualification of the many teachers who attended the course, as 'a Mickey Mouse degree', and was scornful of their work, leading them to feel anxious that they might never reach the required standard. When one of the brightest students, a teacher of forty, expressed her disappointment at not obtaining a distinction for the previous term's work, as she had done the term before, he explained in detail why this was. 'I trust I have made the position quite clear,' he concluded. 'May I add that a little humility on behalf of a student is not unbecoming? You are extremely lucky to be allowed to do an

At Monksfield College.

MA without at least a II (ii) in Theology.' She felt this rebuke to be patronising; had she known that it came from a man who had been admitted to study for an MA despite having no under-graduate degree whatsoever, she might have considered it rich.

Despite the high turnover of staff, Peters found a ready supply of young postgraduates to fill the places of those who left. One such was Mike Higton, who had recently completed a Ph.D. in theology when he received a letter from Peters asking whether he would be interested in teaching at Monkfield. Higton was flattered and excited; he needed the teaching experience (and the money), and in any case was happy to be taken so seriously. He and his wife drove out to Leadenham to meet Peters, who described himself as a retired Anglo-Catholic priest and church historian. The setting was idyllic, the house was rather grand in a faded sort of way, and Peters himself pleasant, with an impish sense of humour. He showed his guests around the site with wide-eyed delight and enthusiasm; he made them feel like co-conspirators in an ambitious but righteous plan to provide theological education to students normally excluded from it. Higton came away thrilled to be involved and eager to help. Because of other commitments he was unable to begin teaching at Monkfield immediately, but in the meantime he drew up module descriptions, helped Peters draw up some syllabus plans and discussed with him the development of a full BA, rather than just a diploma. The Higtons also created a simple website for the college.* During this time, Higton mostly communicated with Peters by telephone (and an occasional email, which he was just beginning to use). He enjoyed working with Peters, who was jovial, encouraging and full of praise. He had no inkling that the man was anything other than what he claimed to be, or that there was anything amiss with the college – to the extent that he felt happy to introduce Peters to a friend of his, who became a teacher at Monkfield. Higton accepted the implicit storyline: that they were fighting the good fight together, doing something noble on a shoestring budget and with a bit of daring, by working outside the constrictions of the Establishment. He had no idea, then, quite how far outside they were.

Towards the end of 1996, De Montfort's Pro-Vice-Chancellor had written to Peters to tell him that, 'following a review of our outreach arrangements', the university would no longer be

---

* On hearing the story of Robert Peters, people invariably comment that 'it couldn't happen nowadays, in the age of the internet'. The evidence suggests otherwise: fraudsters and bigamists seem to be as active today as they have ever been. Indeed such miscreants may benefit from the current cant about 'confidentiality' and 'transparency', causing employers to be more reluctant than they were in the past to provide frank testimonials, particularly when the conduct of an employee has been questionable. Peters himself continued his deceptions into the digital era.

able to accredit the college's courses after the end of the 1996–7 academic year. Questioned about this later, De Montfort's Academic Registrar confirmed that there were 'other reasons' for withdrawing validation, but would not be pressed further. (The Vice-Chancellor had received a confidential letter from Professor Dilks of Hull University.) Peters told Higton that arrangements were being made for Monkfield's courses to be validated by the University of Hertfordshire. Notwithstanding this, Monkfield applied for validation from the University of Sheffield. Peters concealed the fact that De Montfort had withdrawn its accreditation; instead he suggested that Monkfield wanted to withdraw from De Montfort. 'Our Board strongly feels that we ought to seek validation from a long-established university, rather than a 1992 one,' he wrote loftily to Tom Rhodes, Sheffield's Assistant Registrar. He referred to 'our need for an early start date', implying that if this were not possible, they would look elsewhere. A mass of paperwork followed, including a new CV, the usual mixture of truth, half-truth and lies. In the latter category was the old claim that he had sat examinations for the Bar and joined Gray's Inn during a period when in reality he was in prison, serving a sentence for bigamy.

Though Peters had agitated for a speedy decision, it was not until January 1999 that Sheffield sent a team to inspect Monkfield. As well as Rhodes, there were two others: Walter Houston, a member of the Department of Biblical Studies at Sheffield, and Martyn Percy, now director of the Lincoln Theological Institute (part of Sheffield University) and theological assessor on the Board of Collegiate Studies. Peters did a double take when Percy arrived, but neither man acknowledged publicly that they had met before. It became apparent to the visitors that very few students visited the college; teaching took place mostly 'by telephonic communication'. The set-up was painfully amateur, exemplified when Mrs Peters could not find the college accounts to show them. They were introduced to the 'local worthies' on the board of governors. To the team from Sheffield, Monkfield seemed the Fawlty Towers of theological colleges. On the journey back, they were laughing so much at what they had seen that they had to pull over into a lay-by.

Martyn Percy offered to investigate. He telephoned Lambeth Palace and spoke to someone who immediately recognised the name Peters: 'we have a filing cabinet stuffed with documents about him.' While it was true that he had been ordained in the early 1940s, 'everything else is fake'. Meanwhile Percy and his colleagues had been recommended to a professor at Durham, whose advice on Peters was succinct: 'avoid him like the plague.' Through the Durham professor they received the dossier on Peters compiled by Gavin White. Within ten days or so they had learned more than enough to convince them not to proceed further. It fell to Tom Rhodes, Sheffield's Assistant Registrar, to convey the decision to Peters. 'Following discussions with colleagues within the University and at other universities I now have to inform you that we are unable to pursue the validation of your Master's programme,' wrote Rhodes. 'While there are obvious merits to the programme delivered at your institution we are particularly concerned about aspects of your curriculum vitae.'

The decision evoked an indignant response from Peters. 'We are horrified at the inferences contained in your letter of 1 February 1999 and we must ask you to substantiate them,' he wrote. 'This College has a most enviable record of work and achievement and it cannot be blighted by gossip and innuendo.'

A few days later a letter arrived from Mrs Peters, signing herself 'Clerk to the Governors'. She suggested that at least one of the inspectors had arrived at Monkfield 'with his decision already made' – indeed, 'his presence created a very embarrassing situation'. She was referring, of course, to Martyn Percy. 'He and the Principal had been involved in a theological altercation many years ago,' she explained. She warned that 'the College Governors have consulted their legal advisors', who were considering their position. 'The defamatory statement in your letter, and others made by your colleagues, cannot be overlooked.'

Mike Higton was due to begin teaching at Monkfield in two weeks' time when he happened to speak on the telephone to Martyn Percy, whom he knew professionally.* Percy explained that he had been looking into Monkfield and had serious concerns; also that it had become clear to him that Monkfield was not, at that point, validated by any university. In a panic Higton contacted a pro-vice-chancellor at the University of Hertfordshire, who told him plainly that Monkfield's request for validation had never got past a very early stage, that it was unlikely to proceed and that they were therefore unable to assure either him or any of Monkfield's students that validation would happen. One of the Monkfield students contacted Higton to say he had received the same information and was quitting the course. Higton telephoned Peters and (acting on advice from a lawyer friend) insisted that he would only go ahead and teach (he was due to begin in a couple of weeks) if he could assure the students that the course would be validated. Peters responded with

---

* Higton had recently written a favourable review of a book of Percy's in an academic journal.

angry accusation, vitriol and belittlement, and threatened to sue Higton for breach of contract – a threat reinforced two days later by a lawyer's letter. As he had done with others who defied him, Peters tried to coerce Higton into submission by suggesting that he would make it difficult for him to find another job in the relatively small world of academic theology. But Higton stood firm, and his resignation was very grudgingly accepted. Another of the tutors, a postgraduate student studying at Sheffield, also resigned.

In his telephone conversation with Peters, Higton had expressed disquiet about what he had been told about Peters's past. On his part, Peters seemed to believe that Higton was motivated not by the validation issue but by these allegations against him personally, and he insisted, without going into any detail, that he could refute them all, and that there was a laughably ill-informed campaign against him.

All this was fuel to the fire for the Peters family. 'Not only is my husband under attack from the malicious tongues of Sheffield but now some of your libellous statements have a direct bearing on myself,' Mrs Peters wrote in a second letter to Tom Rhodes. 'By maintaining that my husband has been involved in several marriages you are casting a slur on myself.' She summarised the damage done by these supposed slanders: 'By attacking my husband's academic record, all of which is authenticated, and in all of which I have been involved, you are attacking one of the bases of our marriage and our family life.'

A third letter, this time to Dr Houston, was even more emotional in tone. 'If you are looking for a libel action, you are going about it the right way,' she wrote. 'My husband and I have been married since 1960 [sic] and have been together throughout the years since then. If my husband's background were as you are painting it, it is extremely unlikely that his fidelity would have lasted all these years and I resent deeply the imputation that my husband is unfaithful.' Towards its close, the tone of her letter rose to a crescendo:

> We are not prepared to endure your persecution any further. The hypocrisy of your visit to the College is unbelievable. You did not come here with open minds, you came to destroy, behind a façade of 'looking around'.

Mrs Peters's letter was followed by one from a firm of Lincoln solicitors, acting under instruction from the Monkfield board of governors. The solicitor's letter accused Rhodes and his colleagues of bringing the college's reputation into disrepute and insisted on an immediate and full apology. If the situation were not rectified immediately, it warned, 'we can advise that they [the governors] intend to seek redress'.

It was all bluff, of course. After some internal discussion, and a consultation with the professor of law, Rhodes replied, stating that Sheffield University did not accept that any statements had been made which gave rise to any liability in defamation; that in the circumstances the university felt that no apology or retraction was called for; and that the university would vigorously contest any legal action that might arise. None did.

Peters knew that the accusations against him were true. Presumably he hoped to cow his accusers into acceptance of his version of his past. If it came to the test, he would be exposed as a liar. Arguably he had little to lose: having been exposed so many times in the past, he might as well try to bluff it out. But maybe this explanation of Peters's attitude is to misunderstand the psychology of men like him. Perhaps, feeling himself to have been unjustly treated in life and cheated of what he deserved, he felt justified in any action that might help him achieve his ends. And perhaps he had come to believe his own inventions. He was certainly very convincing to others. Higton had finished his telephone call half-persuaded that Peters might be innocent of the accusations against him, despite all that he had heard to the contrary.

As for Mrs Peters, her protestations of her husband's fidelity read oddly, given the evidence of Peters's repeated predatory behaviour towards women; it seemed as if he could scarcely be left alone with a woman without making advances to her. It is hard to believe that his wife could have been unaware of this, or of the fact that her husband had been married several times before. Her assertion that they were married in 1960 – not a slip, because she made the same claim in a different form in another letter, in which she wrote 'I have been married to my husband for 39 years in a thoroughly stable marriage' – is manifestly untrue: records show that they married in September 1966. Had they wed in 1960, the marriage would have been bigamous, because Peters was then married to Marie, the young woman from New Zealand whom he had met in Oxford less than two years before. Marie's son (Peters's only child) was born in March 1960.

To one of the women students on whom he pressed his attentions, Peters intimated that he was about to become a bishop; henceforth he styled himself 'The Right Reverend Dr R. P. Peters'. He appeared at a Mass to mark the Queen's golden jubilee in 2002, by now rather portly, resplendent in purple cassock and biretta and a lace cotta. Peters presented himself as an Anglican priest who had left the Church of England over the issue of the ordination of women and had joined the Old Polish Catholic Church – a small sect, not to be confused with the Roman Catholic Church in Poland. (Unlike many other Churches, the Old Polish Catholic Church is not in communion with the Church of England and its orders are not recognised.) Peters seemed disconcerted to discover that the priest in charge happened to speak Polish, whereas he (as rapidly became apparent) spoke no Polish at all. At the Mass he sat enthroned in a Glastonbury chair on the north-east side of the nave, but the priest did not permit him to carry out any episcopal or priestly function.

To the end, Peters presented the outward appearance of a respectable scholar. For several successive years he attended the annual conference of the Society for Reformation Studies, though his presence caused some embarrassment, especially in 2002, when the conference was held in Cambridge. In that same year a book review appeared under his name in the reputable *Journal of Ecclesiastical History*. The book was a monograph on Thomas Cranmer's doctrine of repentance. The penultimate sentence was especially apposite: 'Will the real Cranmer ever be revealed?'

Following the failure of the application to Sheffield, Monkfield College continued to operate, albeit on a very small scale, with an ever-diminishing number of students and staff. In the academic year 2002–3, for example, the college had just two new students. In 2003 the self-styled bishop and his wife left Leadenham for Corby, Northamptonshire, and then, in 2005, made a final move, to a bungalow in Desborough, near Kettering. For a while Monkfield's courses were validated by the University of Wales, Lampeter, an institution which would be criticised for laxness.* Even this arrangement did not last long, however. In 2001 Peters boasted in a letter to a former member of the Monkfield teaching staff that he had three universities 'on the go', and that a friendly conversation with the Vice-Chancellor of the University of Buckingham had lasted no less than three-quarters of an hour. 'We have heard nothing from Roehampton,' he wrote loftily, 'and a short, sharp note is going there with this mail.' By 2002 the college was offering its own degrees in religious studies and Reformation studies. After exhausting the possibilities in the United Kingdom, Peters forged a link with Kensington University in Hawaii – an institution so disreputable that it was eventually shut down by state authorities. Among its alumni was the late North Korean president, Kim Il-Sung.

A photograph on the Monkfield website, taken around the turn of the century, showed what was termed a 'Congregation', a graduation ceremony. In the foreground a begowned student bowed humbly to receive a worthless diploma, while some functionary waited nearby to drape him with the hood. A handful of other expectant students stood nearby. Overlooking the proceedings was Peters, seated on a throne in glorious apparel – crimson gown and mortar board – his face inscrutable, like an Oriental despot. It was, perhaps, his apotheosis.

---

* Lampeter lost its separate identity in 2009, when it merged with another constituent body of the University of Wales. A Quality Assurance Agency report in 2007 had warned of 'limited confidence' in its management and ability to ensure academic standards.

Epilogue

I started writing this book without being certain that I would be able to publish it. I did not know then whether Robert Peters was alive or dead; and while the latter seemed likely, since (I was almost sure) he was born in 1918, I could not state this with absolute confidence. In my earlier career as a publisher I had heard several alarming stories of books that had to be pulped because people depicted in them had taken offence. I knew of one case in which a book had been pulped not once but twice: first in hardback, after an individual assumed dead had risen, Lazarus-like, and threatened a defamation suit; and then again in paperback, because the editor failed to make the necessary correction. I knew that Peters was litigious, so much so that Trevor-Roper, not normally one to shirk a fight, had been deterred from writing about him. And though I could substantiate most of the damaging information about Peters in the book, there might be something in the story that I would be unable to prove beyond reasonable doubt.

While writing this book, however, I received firm evidence that Peters was no more, in the form of his death certificate (to which I refer in the prologue). Justin Meggitt, more adept than I am at navigating the internet, found this and obligingly sent

The Rt Rev'd Dr Robert Peters
Principal of Monkfield College

FUNERAL SERVICE

2.00pm Tuesday 6th December

Raynham St Martin's
St Martin's church, South Raynham, Fakenham, Norfolk

Flowers to Messrs Canler & Son,, Funeral Directors, Highfield Road, Fakenham, Norfolk, NR21 9DH

it to me. Then, as I was writing the last chapter, I received yet another dossier on Peters, this from someone who had known him during his last few years and had received a notice giving details of a funeral service (which he had been unable to attend); this notice was included in the dossier. It announced that a funeral service was due to take place at 2.00 p.m. on Tuesday 6 December 2005. The deceased was listed as 'The Rt Rev'd Dr Robert Peters, Principal of Monkfield College'. The location was a rural Norfolk church; it seemed possible that Peters had been buried there. Though I live on the other side of the country, I decided to try to find my subject's place of rest. I was particularly interested to see what might be inscribed on Peters's gravestone.

In June 2017 I made a pilgrimage to South Raynham, south-west of Fakenham. Though the area is now sparsely inhabited, there are three churches nearby, all part of the same parish. At the second attempt I found St Martin's, where the funeral had taken place, down a lane that leads nowhere. The church, parts of which date from the early fourteenth century, seemed large for such an isolated rural spot. It was a pleasant spring day, warm and breezy; I searched the churchyard for Peters's gravestone, without success. There was nobody in the church and nobody else around. A notice directed visitors to the warden who lived next door, but the gardener who was working there told me that the owner was away. Having come so far, I decided to take one last look around the churchyard, and then I found it: a humble wooden cross, much smaller and lower than the gravestones, stained and darkened by the damp, with a covering of lichen. Nailed to it was a small metal plaque, with this simple inscription:

Conclusion: Person parson

What kind of man was Parson Peters? Why did he lie so much? Why did he expend so much effort on deceit, when it might have been easier to pursue an honest career? One might argue on his behalf that he became enmeshed in a web of his own lies. Doubtless there is an element of truth in that theory – though he did have opportunities to escape and failed to take them. Why?

Of course it is rash to speculate about the causes of anyone's actions. Nobody can sound the secrets of the human heart. But, in the case of Robert Peters, one can recognise recurrent patterns of abnormal behaviour that are certainly suggestive.

The classic confidence trickster aims to make money by 'conning' other people. Robert Peters was not one of these. Though some of his scams were profitable, plenty of them were not – in fact some of his lies were not really scams in that sense. On the contrary, it seems clear that what Peters wanted most was not money but status. He sought the outward signs of this, as a minister of religion or a doctor of philosophy, in order to obtain respect, admiration, or even, one could say, adulation, from his flock, no matter how small in numbers they might be. He demanded submission from his devotees, and was suspicious of the least sign of independence. It was no coincidence that he treated his wives like skivvies. The top-heavy hierarchy of Monkfield College seemed to most observers ludicrously self-important, but its function was to emphasise his position as Principal. He showed a pronounced liking for ritual, in which he would usually preside, or at least play some significant role. Though he risked exposure, Peters could not resist any opportunity to officiate in church. It was revealing that he created his own private oratory in each of his houses. For Peters, the act of worship was also one of self-worship. In another life, or perhaps another country, he might have become leader of a cult.

Childhood illness may have played some part in shaping his personality. To have been born 'a hopeless cripple' and to have spent the first nine years of his life confined within a steel frame must have been traumatic, especially if his own father rejected him – though we only have Peters's word for all of this, and time and again his word has been shown to be worthless. The whole story may have been no more than a self-justificatory fiction.

Just as he sought to promote his own status, so he showed disdain for those whom he judged inferior to him. He responded to challenges with bullying and threats of litigation. Peters could quickly turn nasty if you came up against him. Those who had been misled into thinking him a kindly old clergyman were often shocked by his invective. His abusive comments about women (and women priests in particular) were especially striking. There was no contradiction between such misogynist slurs and his recurrent lecherous behaviour towards women. How often is it observed that those who are most vociferous in condemning vice are themselves guilty of it?

'Where there is shame, there may yet be virtue,' wrote that wise man, Dr Johnson. So far as we can tell, Peters showed no shame when his misdeeds were exposed and therefore no repentance. He never acknowledged that his actions might be morally wrong or damaging. It was not that he had no understanding of others; in fact he was alert to people's vulnerabilities, shrewdly playing on these to serve his own ends. It seems that, for him, other people existed merely to serve his needs. He did not recognise forgery as criminal or plagiarism as theft. He saw conspiracies against him when none existed. There was logic to his paranoia: if you believe that the world is against you, then maybe lying in your own cause is justified. Feeling hard done by, Peters could imagine that he was righting wrongs done to him by manipulating the facts about his past.

But how could he reconcile his lying with his professed beliefs? Without a conscience, can you be a Christian? However cynical one might be about his motives, it is hard to imagine that a lifetime's religious observance was only for show. Perhaps we can best explain this apparent paradox by suggesting that Peters had lost the capacity to differentiate between truth and falsehood. Being, as he was, so convinced of his rectitude, he could not be telling a lie. On some level Peters believed his own fabrications.

His absolute self-belief made him marvellously plausible, and helps to explain why his deceptions took him as far as they did. Perhaps, too, it explains his evident success with women, despite lacking most of the usually accepted qualities – though it is said that some women are especially susceptible to clerical advances.

While writing about Peters I have often been reminded of another extraordinary confidence trickster, Ronnie Cornwell, whose son David would become the spy novelist John le Carré. Though their personalities were different, yet there were recognisable similarities between the two: in their longing for status, in their unshakeable self-belief, in the ruthlessness with which they exploited others (particularly women), in their lack of remorse. Both men operated in a bewildering variety of guises, across the globe. And, like Robert Peters, Ronnie Cornwell could adopt a sanctimonious persona when it suited him.

Psychiatrists* recognise a condition which they call 'narcissistic personality disorder', with the following features:

- Having an exaggerated sense of self-importance
- Expecting to be recognized as superior even without achievements that warrant it
- Exaggerating your achievements and talents
- Being preoccupied with fantasies about success, power, brilliance, beauty or the perfect mate
- Believing that you are superior and can only be understood by or associate with equally special people
- Requiring constant admiration
- Having a sense of entitlement
- Expecting special favors and unquestioning compliance with your expectations
- Taking advantage of others to get what you want
- Having an inability or unwillingness to recognize the needs and feelings of others
- Being envious of others and believing others envy you
- Behaving in an arrogant or haughty manner

Robert Peters seems a textbook case.

---

* American Psychiatric Association, *Diagnostic and Statistical Manual of Mental Disorders* (fifth edition, 2013).

Chronology

1918 Robert Michael Parkins born in Carlisle on 11
     August, son of James Norman Parkins, solicitor's
     clerk, and his wife, Sophia Sarah, née Edgar.
     Educated at Grosvenor College, Carlisle, and at
     Carlisle Grammar School.

1937–41 Attends St Aidan's Theological College,
     Birkenhead.

1941 Ordained deacon by the Bishop of Wakefield.

1942 Ordained priest. Curate of Almondbury, a village
     near Huddersfield in West Yorkshire.

1943 Marries Hilda Brunton of Warrington,
     schoolmistress (no. 1).

1943–4 Curate of St Mary's, Somers Town, London.

1944 Licence withdrawn by bishop. Begins working for
     the Church Army. Asked to leave a Toc H hostel
     in London after sharing room with psychic.

1945 Teaches at Lord Weymouth's Grammar School,
     Warminster, and acts as chaplain. After a term
     elopes with deputy headmaster's sister-in-law.

1945–6   Takes services in St Alban's, Holborn, and in St
          Paul's Cathedral, London. Teaches at Gresham's
          School, Holt, Norfolk, where he acts as assistant
          chaplain. Dismissed for making improper
          advances to the daughter of a colleague.

1946   Curate of St Columba's Episcopal Church,
          Grantown-on-Spey, in the Scottish Highlands. In
          August marries (bigamously) Margaret Gladdish,
          nurse (no. 2). Arrested and charged with bigamy.
          Sells story to the Glasgow *Sunday Mail* under the
          title 'My Life with Five Women'.

1947   In January jumps bail and flees to Switzerland,
          where he serves briefly as chaplain in the Anglican
          church at Lausanne. Arrested for failing to pay
          a hotel bill and deported to England, but leaves
          train in France and travels to India, via Malta and
          Egypt. Appointed Principal of Anglican Divinity
          School in Ceylon, but does not stay long. Moves
          on to Singapore and then Australia, where he
          teaches at St Peter's College, an Adelaide school.
          Said to have abandoned wife no. 2 on a train.

1948   Possibly deported from Australia. Applies for
          admission to the General Theological Seminary
          in New York, but refused entry visa. Now calling
          himself Robert Parkin Peters, he is re-ordained
          in Canada. Obtains teaching post at Trinity
          College, Toronto, commencing in September.
          Dismissed after only one term as tutor when
          references found to be forged. Crosses border

into America and begins teaching in Pittsburgh; introduces himself to the Bishop of Pittsburgh as the Bishop-elect of Trinidad. Acquires another companion, whom he introduces as his wife (soon discarded). Divorced by wife no. 2.

1949   Teaching in Detroit and Ann Arbor. Divorced by wife no. 1.

1950   Crosses back into Canada and joins Old Catholic sect. Now styling himself Monsignor Peters, he appeals for funds to establish an interdenominational college in the Vancouver area. While seeking work as a teacher in Cloverdale, British Columbia, he offers to validate documents for the university library in Vancouver; these are later found across the border in Seattle, on sale in an antiquarian bookshop.

1950–52   Principal of the Consolidated School of Franklin, Quebec, followed by brief spells teaching in Montreal.

1952   Crosses back into USA. In New York, announces his acceptance of the bishopric of the Leeward Islands – a non-existent post. Acquires vestments on credit. Obtains tutorial post at the College of Wooster, Ohio, thanks to his 'excellent qualifications', especially his degree in history (first-class honours) from Magdalen College, Oxford.

1953   Arrested by the FBI at the College of Wooster on a charge of illegal entry and deported. Afterwards a story about Peters at Wooster, 'The Polished Prof', is published in *Time* magazine. Lands at Plymouth on 11 July and arrested. *Daily Mirror* publishes story: 'Romeo of the Church Swept 7 Women Off Their Feet'. Taken under police guard to Inverness and there sentenced to four months' imprisonment for bigamy. On release, registers with the University of London as an external student for a BA degree in history, but fails the necessary examinations.

1954   Archbishop of Canterbury circulates a memorandum warning about Peters. On 14 August Peters marries Janet Lascelles, widow (no. 3), at the Church of the Annunciation, Bryanston Square, London. Abandons her after only a few days. Proposes marriage to, and is accepted by, four further women over the following year.

1955   Tried at London Quarter Sessions on 23 August on the charge of falsely describing himself as a bachelor. Charge dismissed. Charged the next day with fraudulent conversion and issuing a false cheque, and sentenced to six months' imprisonment. 'Formally and publicly' deprived of his orders by the Bishop of Bath and Wells. On release begins working as secretary for the Bishop of Birmingham. Forges testimonials from Bishop of Birmingham and from the College of Wooster.

1957   Appears at University College, London, claiming to be an MA (Oxon). Halfway through the autumn term, applies to Magdalen College, Oxford, claiming to be a BA (London) and is accepted to read for a B.Litt. (postgraduate) degree.

1958   Marries (bigamously) Marie Baillie (no. 4), postgraduate student, at Lady Margaret Hall, Oxford. Begins officiating at church services around the city. Towards the end of the year, seeks interview with Professor Hugh Trevor-Roper, claiming persecution by the Bishop of Oxford and the President of Magdalen.

1959   Expelled from Magdalen on 29 January. Several stories about him appear in the *Daily Express* and other newspapers. Goes to ground in St Deiniol's Library, Hawarden, North Wales. Applies for various jobs in Britain and abroad, using forged references. Applies to Westminster Cathedral for admission to the Roman Catholic Church (refused). *Sunday Pictorial* publishes story: 'Peters the Parson Clears Out'. Peters sells his story to the *Sunday Pictorial*: 'My Years with Four Women'. Appears in Dublin in the spring and applies for clerical and teaching posts in the Church of Ireland, the Roman Catholic Church and Trinity College, Dublin (all applications unsuccessful). Appointed to teaching post at United College, Winnipeg, but appointment cancelled before he arrives. Appointed to teach at University of

Ottawa beginning in September. Dismissed after a few months for falsifying his references.

1960   Applies to read for a Ph.D. in the universities of Toronto and McGill, but arrested and held in jail in Montreal pending deportation. His son, Gregory, born in March. Takes ship back to Ireland just ahead of a deportation order. Consults psychiatrist. Appointed to post at Leeds, but appointment cancelled when head of department learns the truth about him. Accepted by Professor Gordon Rupp of Manchester University to read for an MA. Ingratiates himself with the Bishop of Manchester and resumes officiating at Church of England services.

1962   Begins to attend academic conferences and publish articles in learned journals.

1963   Granted an MA by Manchester and is accepted to study for a Ph.D. His book *Oculus Episcopi* published by Manchester University Press. Mrs Peters (no. 4) returns to New Zealand with their son, Gregory.

1964   Peters applies for jobs in schools and record offices. Threatens to sue headmaster of Gresham's for cautioning potential employers against him. In October obtains post with the Cambridge Group for the History of Population and Social Structure; its director, E. A. Wrigley, who was Bursar of Peterhouse, obtains college accommodation for him in Fitzwilliam Street.

Discharged in December, but hangs on to college flat. Begins teaching as a tutor in English at a school for overseas students in Eastbourne. Ingratiates himself with vicar's wife and teenage daughter and proposes marriage to the daughter. She accepts, but withdraws when she learns the truth about him. Around this time he marries an unnamed academic at King's College, London (no 5).

1965 In March Mowbrays bookshop in Cambridge complains that Peters has not paid large bills for books obtained on credit. In May the Bishop of Ely warns all clergy against Peters. Peters seeks interview with the bishop, who declines to see him. In September Trevor-Roper is startled to see Peters speaking at an international historical congress in Vienna.

1966 Appointed assistant master at The Leys School, Cambridge, for one term only. In August Rupp recommends Peters for a tutorial post at St Andrews: 'I think he has now established some sort of claim to have his past forgotten, and to be taken on the merits of his performance in the last four years, which has shown a continuing maturing both in his character and in his teaching abilities.' Appears at annual conference of the Catholic Record Society. Disappears from Cambridge, without leaving a forwarding address, when Peterhouse threatens legal action for non-payment of rent on the Cambridge flat, leaving another 'gigantic' unpaid bill to the booksellers Bowes and Bowes. Marries Ann Brinded (no. 6) in Manchester. Leaves hurriedly for America, to take up post as assistant professor at Hope College, Michigan. Applies for posts at the universities of Illinois and Wisconsin; offered posts at University of Texas and American University in Washington. Despite being a Protestant, negotiates to teach at the Catholic University of America in Washington.

1967   Arrested by the FBI and deported after nationwide publicity in print media and on network television. Surfaces in Edinburgh, teaching at a crammer. Blocked from teaching at a girls' school. Appointed part-time lecturer at Northwestern Polytechnic.

1968   Applies to join the Oxford and Cambridge Club. Preaches at St Paul's, Covent Garden. Appointed editor at Gregg International Publishers; threatens to sue when appointment terminated.

1969   Appointed copy editor at Oxford University Press; dismissed after two months. Officiates at church services in Oxford until discovered doing so by the bishop. Applies unsuccessfully for Chair of Social and Cultural History at the University of Malaya.

1970   Fails Ph.D. Appeals unsuccessfully to the Queen. Employed briefly by American University,

Dropmore, Beaconsfield. Attends international historical congress in Moscow and upsets other delegates. Appointed to teach theology by the Open University, but dismissed when his credentials found to be fake.

1971   Appointed to teach at the University of Western Ontario, but appointment cancelled before it started.

1972?   Arrives at the Bible Institute, Birmingham, and is greeted as the answer to their prayers.

1973–8?   Principal of St Aidan's College, Willey, Shropshire.

1974?   Under the name Robert Parkins, accepts post as head of religious education at Aylestone School in Hereford. Bigamously marries colleague named Margaret (no. 7); dismissed when found to have forged qualifications. Regius Professor of Divinity at Cambridge circulates memorandum declaring St Aidan's to be 'wholly undesirable on ecclesiastical, educational and personal grounds'. Cambridge Local Examination Board withdraws its recognition of the college as an examination centre. Peters threatens legal action. Listed as a contributor to the second edition of the *Oxford Dictionary of the Christian Church*.

1975   St Aidan's exposed in *Sunday People* (8 June).

1978   Applies to the Department of Religious Studies in the University of Aberdeen to read for an M.Litt. degree, later upgraded to a Ph.D.

1979   Unsubstantiated report that Peters had married while in Aberdeen (no. 8). Applies for British Academy grant to carry out research in Africa.

1980?   On secondment with the United Society for the Propagation of the Gospel in Malawi.

1981   Obtains Ph.D. from University of Geneva – a theological college in North Carolina. Claims to have been offered a parish in Donegal. Applies to join the Society of Antiquaries in Edinburgh. Reappears in the Manchester area.

1982   Senior lecturer in the Uyo College of Education, Nigeria.

1983   Director of Theological Studies, University College, Buckland. Appears on BBC's *Mastermind*. Exposed in the *News of the World*.

1983–8? In South Africa, initially as Rector of the Anglican church of Virginia, in the Orange Free State – a role he would combine with that of Director of Post-Ordination Training for the diocese of Bloemfontein; causes 'pastoral havoc'. Moves to parish of Bethlehem and then Ladybrand. Lecturer, Federal Theological Seminary, Edendale, Natal; dismissed. Appointed Rector of Vryheid, one of the largest towns in the region bordering the Indian Ocean now known as KwaZulu-Natal; dismissed at the church door for defying canonical authority. Lecturer at a Bible college in the small town of Hebron, north-west of Pretoria. Dismissed and deported back to England.

1988   Applies for reader's ticket at Cambridge University Library. Often to be seen at Tyndale House, Cambridge.

1988?–   Principal of Cambridge Religious Studies Centre, Cambourne, Cambridgeshire. Courses accredited by University of Hull; accreditation withdrawn. Courses accredited by De Montfort University; accreditation withdrawn.

1994?   Cambridge Religious Studies Centre relocates to Buckden, Huntingdonshire.

1995?   Cambridge Religious Studies Centre relocates to the outskirts of Oxford and is renamed Monkfield College.

1996   Monkfield relocates to Leadenham, Lincolnshire.

1997   Monkfield applies to University of Sheffield for
–2000?   accreditation; refused. Peters threatens legal action. Obtains accreditation from the University of Wales, Lampeter; withdrawn. Obtains accreditation from Kensington University, Hawaii.

2000?   Styles himself a bishop in the Old Polish Catholic Church.

| 2003 | Monkfield relocates to Corby, Northamptonshire. |
| 2005 | Monkfield now moribund. Mr and Mrs Peters relocate to Desborough, Northamptonshire. Peters dies 25 November, aged eighty-seven. Funeral at St Martin's, South Raynham, Norfolk. |

Acknowledgements

My first debt is an obvious one: to Hugh Trevor-Roper, whose research informed this book and indeed forms much of its subject. I felt his hand on my shoulder as I wrote, and I like to think that he would have enjoyed the finished product. I owe particular thanks to his literary executor, Blair Worden, for permission to use material from the Dacre archive and for his encouragement throughout. Blair read the typescript and provided helpful comments – as also did Chuck Elliott, Felicity Marris, Justin Meggitt, William Price, Charlotte Sisman, Nicholas Taylor, Simon Winchester and Henry Woudhuysen. Each of them has contributed significantly to improving the book and I am grateful to them all. I must stress, however, that responsibility for any errors in it is entirely mine.

Another of those who read the book at an early stage was Alan Bennett, who was kind enough to recommend it to one of his own publishers, Profile. It has been a pleasure to work with Andrew Franklin and his team, and I want to acknowledge my debt in particular to Cecily Gayford, my excellent editor; and to Lesley Levene, my keen-eyed but flexible copy-editor; and to Profile's managing editor Penny Daniel, who has patiently and skillfully seen the manuscript through the stages of production.

I am grateful to the following individuals for their help in various ways: Paul Ayris, David Bagchi, David Bacon, Anthony Bash, Edward Bundock, David Dilks, Bill Domeris, Peter Doyle, Graham Duncan, Stella Fletcher, Leslie Francis, Sheridan Gilley, Lester Grabbe, Peter Harland, Ian Hazlett, Mike Higton, Philip Johnston, Anthony Leeper, Jane McLarty, John Marmion, Sarah Maxwell, Peter Oppenheimer, Martyn Percy, Frederick Ratcliffe, Tom Rhodes, Graddon Rowlands, Bryan Spinks, Tom Stanage, Nick Thompson, Andrew Walls, Rodney Ward, Doug Wessels and his daughter Lyn. I owe a special debt to Gavin White, whose pursuit of Peters was second only to the professor's.

I want to acknowledge the help of various archivists: Judith Curthoys, Christ Church, Oxford; Ben Taylor, Magdalen College, Oxford; Liz Larby, Gresham's School, Norfolk; James Peters, University of Manchester Library; Mike Harkness and Richard Higgins, Special Collections, University Library, Durham; Helen Price, Brotherton Library Special Collections, Leeds; Andrea McKinnon-Matthews, St Peter's College, South Australia; Sylvia Lassam, Trinity College, Toronto; and Andrew Mussell, Gray's Inn. I also wish to acknowledge help from Clare Davidson, administrator, King's College, University of Aberdeen; Mark Mortimer, headmaster, and Stella Aldridge, Deputy Head of Development and Alumni Relations, Warminster School (formerly Lord Weymouth's Grammar School); and Andrew Rattue, Principal of St Clare's.

I am grateful to Alan Samson of Weidenfeld & Nicolson for permission to reproduce two passages (albeit modified) from my biography of Hugh Trevor-Roper, published in 2010.

Lastly I should like to thank my agent, Andrew Wylie, and his colleague Tracy Bohan, for their encouragement and support.

Index

Page references for footnotes are followed by n

List of Illustrations

Picture Credits

Author's photograph 199; Frank Hudson/Associated Newspapers 83; Mirrorpix 46, 95, 139; Peterhouse College 145; Trevor-Roper dossier 20, 51, 53, 66, 88, 104, 110, 120, 123, 133, 142, 151, 152, 159, 187, 198.

ADAM SISMAN is the author of *Boswell's Presumptuous Task*, winner of the National Book Critics Circle Award for Biography, and the biographer of John Le Carré, A. J. P. Taylor, and Hugh Trevor-Roper. Among his other works are two volumes of letters by Patrick Leigh Fermor. He is a fellow of the Royal Society of Literature and an honorary fellow of the University of St Andrews.